SONG OF MOVING WATER

Also by Susan Schmidt

Salt Runs in My Blood

Landfall on the Chesapeake, in the Wake of Captain John Smith

SONG OF MOVING WATER

Susan Schmidt

for David

Susan

Kakapo Press
Beaufort, North Carolina
2015

Kakapo Press
susu@susanschmidt.net
www.susanschmidt.net

ISBN 13-978-0-9863835-1-9
ISBN 10-0-9863835-1-1

Credit: "Black Waters" by Jean Ritchie © 1967, 1971
Geordie Music Publishing Co, All Rights Reserved.
Used by Permission.

Cover painting is by Kim Hall, kimhallstudio.com

Author photo by Anne Smith Mahoney

For my godchildren

The Sound of Mountain Water
—Wallace Stegner

1

Clouds of apple blossoms in the hillside orchard scented the sky around Grace, and old-timey fiddle tunes played in her head. Where she sat on the western slope, spring-green leaves were just catching the first light. Farm fields filled the narrow valley to the edge of the river. Across the river to the east, the green timbered hill rose sharply three thousand feet to block the morning sun. Her eye followed the wooded slope straight down to the river, across eroded folds of pastures to the road, house, and garden. Parked by the cowbarn and chicken coop was Ruby's half-long yellow school bus. The hayfields below and orchards around Grace were gone to meadow flowers, and behind her up the hollow was National Forest and West Virginia. Her view of pastures, sheds, and the old white house was a patchwork of memory.

Early this morning, Grace had driven three hours to the farm and now was hungry. No one was home in the farmhouse when she had knocked on the door, so she climbed the hill to wait. In a pocket she found a Milky Way bar and gobbled it. She sensed a source of strength from the chocolate and from the hill. She was born in this landscape, and the spirit of her family and homeplace began to awake in her.

Since her father's death seven years earlier, Grace had not returned to McDowell County. Every year she received a birthday card from her Aunt Ruby, but, since she was ten, she had not seen her aunt. Now her stepfather Tolly wanted to sell her father's farm, where Aunt Ruby lived. She recalled Ruby's letter, which she had received a week earlier, addressed to her full name, Grace Dabney McAuley. The letter raised her curiosity to renew ties with her father's family.

"*Since I broke my leg and can't get around,*" Ruby's letter read, "*I've been staying up the road with the Bentons. Your mother's new husband wants me to move into the Methodist nursing home in Staunton. To afford that, I'll have to sell off the furniture. You surely are welcome to anything you want, but unless I hear from you, I'll just go ahead and sell the farm tools and your Daddy's things too, as Mr. Tolliver instructed me. The farm is yours, you should already know, on your eighteenth birthday, in July this year. Your Daddy left it to you, with me being able to stay as long as I live. But Mr. Tolliver says you want to sell whenever I can move out."*

Grace was irked that her stepfather, Horace Taliaferro, as executor of her father's will, had never told her the truth—first, that she owned the farm and, second, that he had asked Ruby to move. Apparently, when Grace was eighteen in four months, the farm would be hers. So she decided to check out her father's land.

As a senior at St. Catherine's School in Richmond, Grace was supposed to sleep in the dorm when her mother and stepfather were away, and they were always travelling. She had told the dorm mother she was going home for the weekend, which stretched the truth, but her true home really was on Jack Creek in McDowell County and not in Richmond.

On Friday night a taxi had dropped Grace in the crescent driveway of her mother's house off Cary Street, and she dumped her duffel of clothes and books by the walnut banister in the front hall. "Eleanor, Tolly," she yelled. In Virginia, her stepfather's name was pronounced Tolliver, and like her mother, Grace called him Tolly instead of Horace.

In her room in the empty house Grace fell asleep and opened her eyes Saturday morning at the blare of an alarm. Before daylight she showered and pulled on flowered cotton slacks, a peach shirt, and brown sweater—clothes hanging in her closet that Eleanor had bought her. Grace was five feet, four inches, a sturdy field-hockey halfback—more jock than ballerina. She tugged a brush through bushy, rusty-brown hair that hung below her shoulders. Eleanor had said that Grace's hair was her best asset if she would tend it; but Eleanor also said that she had thick peasant's ankles from her father.

In the early dark Grace threw the duffel in her car parked

behind the house. She had just bought the new 1975 gray Toyota station wagon with money inherited from her grandmother Charlotte Dabney. A denim jacket was on the backseat; her stepbrother Jared must have been driving her car. Leaving Richmond just after five-thirty in the morning, in the dark she drove Interstate 64 West past Charlottesville. In Staunton, on two-lane Route 250 she stopped at a truck stop for hot chocolate and a gooey-sweet honeybun for breakfast. She downshifted to climb the western ridge of the Shenandoah Valley to the Confederate Breastworks in time to watch sunrise spread over farms to the east behind her. Early April was cooler at the higher elevation, and Grace put on Jared's jacket over her sweater when she got out to look as the sun cast pink light over hills and valleys to the west where she was heading.

The road west snaked down the slope of Shenandoah Mountain. Grace still had to drive another hour through McDowell County, winding up and over three more ridges, crossing narrow valleys of the Bullpasture, Calfpasture, and Cowpasture rivers. Some awakening part of her remembered to turn left in Jackson by the Feed and Seed store. Twelve miles south of town she turned north across the bridge by the white church, up Jack Creek Valley. Sheep grazed in pastures on steep hillsides. She passed the little general store with the unpainted porch directly on the road, the faded red and yellow school-bus shelter stenciled with snuff advertisements, where she had stood out of the rain, to this old white frame house with the mailbox marked "McAuley."

Where Grace sat on the hill above the house, the sun over the ridge dried dew on clover in the orchard. Down the hill she watched the creek sparkle under the footbridge between the house and barn. Beyond the road, across the pasture, the river rolled on by the foot of the opposite hill. As sun warmed her bones, she stood and stretched. Below her she watched pickup trucks parking along the road and a crowd gathering around the white house.

The scene spread below reminded Grace of Brueghel's painting of colorful country folk. She had spent fall semester of

3

twelfth grade at a British boarding school. On a bicycling weekend in the Cotswolds, she had slept in a haybarn with English students. Virginia's foothills looked just like the Cotswolds, or was it the other way around?

Grace was curious about her father's homeplace, but afraid to be disappointed. She had idyllic memories as a little girl, but really didn't remember very much. Down in the yard were the neighbors—Bentons, Dorsets, and Huffmans—and surely her Aunt Ruby. Grace was intrigued to see her old aunt, whom she had not seen for so long. She could faintly remember the woman's calm industry. Would these people she barely remembered recognize her?

Her hair was tangled, and she had no brush. She shook her head, then put on a rubber band to keep unruly rusty curls from her face. She had not locked her car by the shed where people were now milling around, so she started down the sheep path. And she was still hungry.

Grace had been to estate auctions in Williamsburg with Tolly, who collected Oriental rugs and antique silver. Once, when she was eleven, he had let her bid on a china doll, and when she yelled out, "Fifty dollars," the auctioneer slammed down his gavel, "Sold," despite higher bids behind her. "Sold," the auctioneer had said again with emphasis. He would lose no money by his courtesy to the child. Tolly spent lots of money at the auction; Eleanor's money, she thought.

At an estate auction there's a decorum that no one who is local bids against an heir. Word gets around that some niece wants the cut-glass pitcher or another cousin wants a mirror. Generally folks at auctions conspire by not bidding against each other. However, one or two antique dealers from DC or Charlottesville inflated prices for handmade quilts and woven rugs. Grace did not expect to find anything valuable or indispensable at her family's auction. She had no intention of claiming anything.

As Grace walked down the hill between the chicken coop and the granary, she surveyed the crowd, wondering which old lady was Ruby. Local ladies dressed up in Saturday-best, cotton-print dresses, and the men wore clean denim or tan work shirts and pants. Country people must live hard physical lives, she thought, without much culture—no movie theatres or plays or symphony. Eleanor had said little but complaint about living here for ten years. Grace mumbled to herself, "I don't ever want to be poor or bored."

The couples in pastel sportswear like hers were city people from their weekend homes or from the Homestead resort in Bath County. Grace worried what the local people would think of her; were her flowered pants too colorful? Eleanor had drilled that appearance was all that mattered. Grace suppressed her nerves and composed her face. No one would guess she was shy, because she covered her feelings so well.

Grateful to be anonymous, Grace walked along the rows of furniture lined up by roomfuls for people to inspect. In the living-room row were a brown-plaid sofa, an overstuffed yellow chintz chair with worn armrests, a walnut side chair with a split-oak seat, a big console TV, a magazine rack with *National Inquirers* and *Mountain Gazette*, the McDowell County weekly newspaper.

To one side, a kitchen table with a red-checked vinyl tablecloth had a toaster and paper-napkin rack as if just carried outdoors for breakfast. In the next row, piled on bedframes and mattresses, were primary-color rag rugs, quilts, and bedspreads. On top of a clothes bureau was a framed picture of blue-eyed Jesus. Spread out on the wagons by the sheds were several lifetimes of farmers' tools, grass scythes and hayracks, a seed drill, and cracked leather bridles. The tools by the shed were her granddaddy's.

"Old tools teach the hand how to do a job," said an ancient man in bib overalls, hefting a brace and bit. His wizened wife in a calico housedress clutched a cast-iron muffin tin.

Rusting metal parts to fit and fix any machine filled wooden crates printed "McAuley APPLES." An apple box could be a table in her dorm room, Grace thought. There were barrels of bolts, bails of wire, a rifle, knives, and moldy black lace-up shoes. A

5

cook's kitchenware covered the table tops: baking pans; heavy crocks for sauerkraut; cases of canning jars filled with green beans, tomatoes, and corn, taken from their sorting shelves in a root cellar. Beside the salt-glazed butter churn were a tin candlemold and a flowered porcelain chamber pot.

Grace mingled with the curious old ladies, handling the tools and looking through boxes. One woman in knee socks and rubber boots wore an apron still wet from washing breakfast dishes. A little towhead girl ran around underfoot. Grace peeked in a pillowcase of fabric scraps and cheesecloth bags of feathers. Unfinished embroidery on tea cloths and aprons spilled out of a cardboard box. Strewn around the ground were boxes of plates and glasses, pitchers, and lamps. In one bowl she touched a pair of wire-rimmed spectacles. She had inherited nearsightedness from this family.

Grace lifted a quilt folded on top of a box and stooped to read titles of her father's dusty, dark textbooks. One was *English Romantic Poetry*. Where could she store his literature books? She knew Eleanor did not want Tom McAuley's stuff in her Richmond house.

When the auctioneer, elevated on the truckbed, banged his gavel for attention, ladies huddled closer to his bright red pickup. The cab door said, "Harold Hise, Farm Auctioneer, Elkton, VA," with a phone number. Farmers in jeans moved to the back to chew on pipe stems, boast of sharpshooting, and eye Red Velvet cake wrapped in cellophane. At the snack table Grace bought a piece of dark cake and a red pint-carton of milk.

Harold Hise called the crowd's attention again. "We'll start over here with the settee." Several old men stood up from the brown-plaid sofa. Harold Hise rolled off his patter, "Give me thirty dollars for this fine old couch; give me thirty; well, let's start at twenty. Who'll give me twenty dollars? I have two; give me five; okay, three. On my left, three. Going once, going twice, sold for three dollars."

The county folk gathered to socialize; not to buy, but to see what the gear in their own closets and sheds would bring. They knew the things in their lives did not have as much value as their land. But the day was fine, clouds flying, the first crisp ring of spring in birdsong.

Grace glanced up at the auctioneer's assistant, maybe his son, in a white T-shirt with a pack of Camels rolled in the sleeve. He stood by a stuffed chair with a bedspread covering holes where the stuffing bulged, which finally got a bid of one dollar. An unlit cigarette hung from the boy's lips the whole time.

Rifling through a box, Grace found framed grade-school certificates and stiff paired portraits of ancestors in prim black clothes. Underneath was a sepia photo of her father Tom at five, in a white lacy dress and long pale ringlets. She remembered him when he was thirty with black curly hair. He had told her he was once a little girl like her but had kissed his elbow. At five she had tried and tried to kiss her own elbow, but could not bend her arm around. She slipped the photograph of her father into her jacket pocket.

Growing up, Grace would rather have been a boy because Eleanor expected her to behave properly—keeping clean, dressing up, and then getting married, having babies, and keeping house. But Grace didn't know yet what she wanted to do instead.

The auctioneer's assistant opened the doors of a heavy dark armoire lined with pink-flowered wallpaper. He pulled out a music case and held up the instrument inside.

Harold Hise harangued, "Who wants to open? What am I bid on this fine fiddle? Will anybody play a tune? Give me . . . ."

Grace suddenly recognized the fiddle. Irish jigs and reels frolicked in her head from her father's play parties. Startling herself, she called out, "That's my Daddy's fiddle." The auctioneer's rat-a-tat voice poised mid air; the crowd swung half turns in one arc as time suspended.

"I am Grace Dabney McAuley," she said quietly, explanation enough, as she walked up to claim it. She did not show her fear. "I am Grace," she said, nervous, head high, for that was her name when she had lived here. The farm people stared at her, an apparition till now invisible.

Her father had named her Grace for the hymn. He would greet her—singing "Amazing Grace" full bellow—embarrassing her, but she loved it. To Grace, her father singing by himself sounded like three-part harmony. Her middle name was her mother's maiden name. Her parents were so different from each other; these were her own two contradictory halves.

She reached for the fiddle and smoothed her hand over the golden-brown grain of its wood. Two of four strings were missing. This frail box that made music in her childhood released flooding memories dammed up inside her. When her father had fiddled in the kitchen, tapping his toe like a hoedown, like as not, their neighbor Amos would be step-dancing, clowning and slapping his knees.

Grace's name had stopped the momentum of the auction. The brittle moment broke like a river's spring thaw. Curiosity to see Tom McAuley's daughter overcame country shyness. "Well, I'll be." "Pretty as a picture." Neighbors clustered around to greet her. Grace recognized faces, but no names. She smiled self-consciously, still gripping the neck of the fiddle.

"Jess like your Daddy," some old man said.

Grace remembered the porch of the general store down the road where she had walked with her Daddy for a Coke on Saturday mornings. These old men would each ask just to hear her answer, "Who are you like, Gracie?" And she would drawl, "Jess like mah Daddy," and they'd laugh. And her father would glow with pride.

"Who are you like?" "Jess like mah Daddy."

"Young lady, are you authorized to interrupt the auction?" Harold Hise asked. "Mr. Taliaferro instructed me . . . ."

"Yes, I can stop the auction, and I am. I own the farm and everything here, or will soon," Grace said. "Mr. Taliaferro does not."

"Well, all right," the auctioneer said. Talking to his microphone again, he announced, "Miss Grace McAuley says folks

8

can return, or keep, what they already bid on if they want, but the rest of the sale has come to a close." And he banged his gavel a last time.

People there just for the auction filtered away as the morning turned into a celebration. The church ladies passed around egg-salad sandwiches and the Red Velvet cake for free.

"Well, I'll be, Gracie, what an entrance!" exclaimed a young woman, moving slowly through the crowd. At first glance, she was quite fat, but with an air of vitality. Grace immediately recognized her best friend from grade school, two years older, and felt relief at finding someone she knew.

"Hello, Sally Bee Mullins." Grace laughed in amazement. "You're pregnant."

"I'm not Mullins anymore. I'm Sally Pollock."

"You're married?"

"I hope so." Sally Bee laughed, patting her stomach. "This is our second."

As they sat on the sofa to talk, Grace cradled the fiddle in its case. "You married Timothy Pollock in your class?" she asked.

"No. No, Tim's dead," Sally Bee said softly. She whistled a two-tone note, and the towhead, two-year-old girl appeared running among people's feet. "I married his brother Waller. This is Loretta, our little girl. Waller's got her trained to come like a bird dog." Sally Bee was smiling like sunshine.

"You mean, Wally who is ten years older than you?"

"Yes, we got married almost three years ago," Sally Bee said. "He's a mechanic at the tractor factory in Staunton."

Grace didn't feel anywhere near old enough to finish high school, much less get married.

"Loretta plays here all the time. Ruby's like her grandmother."

The two young women stood so the men could move the sofa back into the house. Farmers carried armchairs to the sitting room and bedframes and bureaus upstairs. They dragged up springs and mattresses and plopped them in place.

"Sally Bee, did you drop out of high school?" Grace asked.

9

"I don't need a degree for raising babies."

Grace thought to herself, Eleanor always warned that too much education scares off men.

"Don't rightly know where all those boxes are supposed to go," one man said. "Howdee, Miss Grace, I'm Enoch Conway." His bulging stomach strained the buttons of his plaid shirt.

Sally Bee walked away and returned with a box of cooking utensils. "I felt bad about buying these, but Ruby helped teach me to cook. She'll want them back."

"Don't carry that, Miss Sally Bee," said Charlie, taking the box from her, limping to the house.

"Don't fuss, Charlie. I'm not due for six weeks."

A slight dark man tipped his hat to Grace. "How do? I'm Aaron Miller, three farms north."

As the neighbor men finished piling boxes of books and linens in the back hall, Grace overheard, "Don't you reckon Miss Ruby can move home, now that her niece isn't selling off?"

2

Grace would have recognized Ruby anywhere. Just over five feet tall and thick in the middle, without much neck, with a square jaw and short steel-gray hair—she resembled a hedgehog, or rather a woodchuck; no hedgehogs in America. Grace thought, that's what I'll look like in forty years; why didn't I inherit my father's long legs? Where Tom McAuley had been tall and skinny, Ruby was round and short. She was fourteen years older than Grace's father, and his half-sister.

After the auction, Grace escaped the chaos of boxes at the farmhouse. She found Aunt Ruby in Clara and Harry Benton's doublewide trailer up the road, and she stayed to dinner. Harry was Ruby's first cousin on her mother's Benton side.

Ruby said, "I slipped on the ice first of March hauling buckets of sap to the sugaring shack in the stand of maple trees. Amos come along at dusk to sample the syrup and found me lying there, near frozen." Even laid up with the leg cast, Ruby had arm muscles that Grace had never seen in a woman, let alone an old lady.

Harry said, "Amos drove Ruby in her pickup over here, and I drove her to the University Hospital in Charlottesville."

Ruby added, "Amos slept in my room there two days watching the doctors until I was released." Her accent had the Elizabethan country twang that Eleanor had struggled to erase from her daughter's voice.

"I watched you stop the auction, Grace," Clara said. "Ruby wouldn't go."

"I wasn't going to watch them sell off the family things," Ruby said. "Get on with it, whatever needs to get done, I said, but I'm not going to watch."

"Tolly was wrong to ask you to move," Grace said, marveling at the old lady's forthrightness. "You come back into the house and stay there."

"Ruby still needs waiting on," Clara said, wiping wet hands on

11

her apron, "even though she won't admit it."

Without hesitation, Grace spoke up, "I'll look after you, Ruby." She felt certain that she had made the right decision.

"Well, tables do turn," Ruby said. "I took care of you when you was a baby. Much as I appreciate your hospitality, Clara," Ruby said, "I'm hankering to be off on my own again." Her cheeks bulged when she grinned.

"Well, I've been in heaven with two cooks in the house," Harry said. "Ruby, we'll drive you home after church tomorrow."

Ruby confided to Grace, "Clara puts too much salt in her cooking. It drives me stir-crazy cooped up in her kitchen, especially when I can't tell her what she's doing wrong."

Accustomed to running her own farm, Ruby was riled at the big leg cast, its size calculated to keep her in one place. While she had to sit still, she cut fabric swatches into quilt squares. "You know you can't cut cloth on a Sunday," Ruby said, "or you'll never finish sewing what you start. So I'm cutting what I need for two days. But I can sew tomorrow." Ruby mail-ordered bags of remnants from a mill to sew together into quilt tops. Grace thought polyester was tacky, and the too-bright colors looked like cereal boxes or cartoon shows.

Back in Ruby's old farmhouse Grace was not spooked by staying alone. She felt calmer alone in the country than in a city. She breathed some sense of coming home, like the cinnamon of fresh-baked cookies. This is my father's house, she said to herself. She had come from this valley of green pastures shadowed by timbered hills.

Saturday night, Grace called the Princess Anne Club at Virginia Beach, and George the bartender found Eleanor and Tolly at dinner. George had served Grace lemonade for years, when she came up to the bar after tennis matches, looking for some company.

Over the phone Tolly said, "It's best for me to sell the McDowell County property right away. I have the sale all arranged."

"No," Grace said, even though she was an inconvenience to her stepfather.

"But this business must wait," he said. "I have a golf match tomorrow. Speak to your mother."

"Hello, Eleanor; how are you? I'm going to live with Ruby in her farmhouse." Grace never called her—"Mother."

"Good gracious, child, did you drop out of school?" Eleanor sounded almost glad.

"Oh no, I'm way ahead. I can finish the semester and graduate if I send in one last paper in May." With good grades came privilege.

"You're being foolish, absolutely daft," Eleanor trilled. She warned Grace not to have a flat tire on a mountain road. She had learned long ago to tune out her mother. Too tired to play her mother's guilt-trip games, she said goodnight and hung up the phone on the wall in the farmhouse kitchen.

At the back of the house, the kitchen was the most lived-in room. Neighbors paying a visit always sat at the kitchen table, while Ruby kept on paring or chopping. Jars of preserves and vegetables lined the pantry closet beside the kitchen. Back in place after the auction, in the long narrow back hall were a freezer chest, washer, racks for work coats, shelves for rubber boots, feed buckets, and vegetable baskets.

The unheated back hall led to the bathroom; her father had added indoor plumbing for Eleanor to live there. The only heat in the bathroom came through the open window above the bathtub on the kitchen wall. Anyone standing at the stove could see into the bathroom, unless the curtains were pulled closed.

Beyond the kitchen, downstairs were a small cluttered sitting room and Ruby's bedroom. At the top of the stairs were the two bedrooms where Grace and her parents had slept. As a child, she would creep down the stairs to nestle in Ruby's bed when her father and mother yelled at each other.

When Grace carried her duffel of clothes from the car, two tiny green toads were suctioned onto the back-door window. With

13

the light behind them from the inside, they were translucent.

"Goodnight, little frogs," she said.

In an auction box in the back hall she found a tattered quilt around a lamp she wanted for reading. Turning over books, Grace found a hand-bound notebook in her father's handwriting.

On the stairs her feet remembered the uneven lift of each step. When she walked into her room in the dark, she reached instinctively for the light cord. Over the bare mattress she stretched musty sheets and the quilt. As Grace got in her bed upstairs, dizzy as if from jet lag, she remarked how much noise there was in the silence. Tree toads buzzed from the low-ground along the river. Listening, she could faintly hear the river rolling along and bobbing above the rocks.

Late into the night, wrapped in the quilt, Grace read her Daddy's poems about radiance, shining skies, morel mushrooms chiming in oak leaves. Words played like musical notes of her father's imagination, and she hummed tunes to the rhythm of his mountain phrases.

Her father had never been that handy, except with words. Dreamer, Eleanor had called him, scalawag, spinner of tales. Grace remembered his bedtime stories of wild animals, tree spirits, and river sprites.

"Listen," he would whisper before she fell sleep. "Who cooks for you? Who cooks for you all?" he hooted out the window, and the old barred owl that roosted in the beech tree would hoo-hoo back. "He's saying goodnight to you," her Daddy told her. "Hoo-hooo," she would hoot. In the summer dusk, she whistled three syllables at the whippoorwill, *wher-wher-it*, the middle tone like a grace note, sounding pretty good because the bird always answered as long as she did, leaning out her upstairs window gazing confidently into the dark, with her father anchoring her.

In Grace's dream that first night back in the farmhouse, three people approached her, each bearing a gift. The first was an odd man dressed in gray who said: "Remember where you come from."

The second speaker in the dream, a smiling woman with a

14

shiny halo of wispy white hair was Mrs. Foster, the headmistress of Grace's school in Richmond. She said: "Trust your intuition."

The third who approached in the dream was a young woman Grace had met in France at New Years. This woman at the Taizé monastery sang with the same resonance and started songs at the same pitch as Grace. She said: "I give you your voice."

Half awake, Grace listed the three gifts: her memory, her feelings, and her ability to sing.

3

On the front porch Sunday morning, Grace sat still for a minute while putting the house in order before Ruby came home. She wore baggy jeans that were hanging in the back hall. After the auction, the neighbors had known pretty much in which rooms to put the furniture, but Grace had no clear idea where to empty all the boxes.

Enjoying the view of the river, she mused she might like to be a farmer. A "gentleman farmer," as her stepbrother Jared would say. Live in the country, read, walk, feed some animals, watch the sunset. And drive to Charlottesville for the library and "culture."

A red bird moved in the yard. Grace looked up. No, it was an old man at the gate. He approached silently as not to startle her. Tree bark he looked like. Gray-green and rumpled like lichen, his clothes had been part of him for years, with the same pale hue as his hair and skin. She had not noticed him standing by the tree until he took off his red cap and the color moved like a cardinal from a branch.

"Miss Gracie, I'm Amos Cameron, your next-to neighbor just north, and Clara Benton's brother."

Tall and skinny like her father, Amos was his best friend. This man had step-danced to her father's fiddle and carried her on his shoulders through the woods.

"How do you do, sir?" Grace said. Years before, his weathered face had looked older than the hills to her, but he had not aged since.

"I've come to help you push Ruby's furniture back in place," he said, "since she'll be home this afternoon."

"Sure, thank you, Mr. Cameron, I appreciate your help."

"Call me Amos," he replied, smiling.

While they worked together in the sitting room, the phone rang in the kitchen. It was Ruby.

"Harry's gone off to Staunton," Ruby said over the line. "And

Clara's asked me to stay with her another night. Harry will drive me down tomorrow midday. Come over with Amos at noon for dinner."

"Well, Gracie," Amos said, after they had organized Ruby's bedroom too, "come walk with me to see your Daddy's woods."

In the yard they passed the metal-sheathed shack that housed the tractor and the shed where several cords of wood were stacked to season. They traversed the hill through the orchard, to the hollow where the creek flowed out of the woods. Along the creekbank, ferns bent over the steep path. Grace stayed quiet when Amos did.

He turned from the creek-bed path up a steeper slope into the woods and stopped when they reached a grove of half-grown hickory trees.

"That's a redhead," he looked toward a tap-tap woodpecker-sound and took off his own red cap to scratch his head. She had never seen anybody else with such big rough hands and such big ears.

Amos checked a young tree. He said, "This is a yearling chestnut. Look at the leaf. See this jagged edge like teeth; dentated means toothed. Used to be the main tree in the Virginia mountains before the blight."

Grace slipped the serrated leaf in her pocket. Amos gleaned his wisdom from watching how the woods work rather than from school lectures and church sermons. Ruby was at church right then, Sunday morning.

"It's real sad," Amos mourned. "This yearling tree will die soon from the blight. Your Daddy used to say, 'If I could see something within my lifetime, I'd like to see chestnuts come back full grown in the hills.' You know, the woods used to be full of chestnuts. The chestnut blight was the worst thing that hit us," Amos said.

"Why did they disappear?" she asked.

"The disease killed off all the chestnut trees in the Appalachian mountains," Amos said. "Some infected trees from

China brought the blight to the World's Fair, and it traveled along the mountain chain from Canada to Georgia. Right about when we were born, your Daddy and me, all the chestnut trees here started dying. Growing up, we watched big trees like this one fall."

Amos walked over and sat on a downed tree trunk, pulled out his knife, and whittled away at a stick. Grace sat next to him.

"This big chestnut log is still hard as iron, though it fell fifty years ago. Folks used to build fence posts and doorsills out of chestnut," he said. "The wood would never rot."

The tree trunk was the right height for a seat and worn where someone had sat a long time. The two sat still for a while. Amos whittled away slivers of wood, carving with the grain, until bird beak, wings, and feathers started to emerge from the basswood stick. His big hands were agile. In the city, no one stayed quiet if there was nothing to say.

Watching Amos whittle, after a while she asked, "Are there any big chestnut trees now?"

"Saplings still grow up from underground roots for a year or two, then die off." Amos smoothed the wood he was carving. "Nuts rolling down a hill would pile knee-deep behind a log. You could scoop 'em up by the barrel-full. Chestnuts would feed animals, Indians, and settlers," he said. "Wasn't any need for money with nuts ground for flour meal."

Grace pictured this slope full of Indians scooping up chestnuts with blue plastic garbage cans.

"Woodpecker," he said, handing her the stick he had been whittling. She held the bird in her palm for a while, then put it in her pocket as they walked.

"What are all these trees?" she asked. Sun filtered through the light-green dome above them.

"Maple, oak, hickory, tulip poplars, dogwood." Amos spread his arms out at the trees growing all around them. "But nothing grew as tall and fine as chestnuts.."

Under her feet, green plants of many shapes peeped from the brown moist forest floor. Following behind Amos, Grace noticed flowers in the herby undergrowth along the path.

"What're these?" she asked, pointing to three-leaf, three-petal flowers.

"Trillium," he said. "They come red, speckled. These white ones turn pink as they get old." Grace leaned down, touching the trillium. "You're going to college, right? Why don't you study trees and find the cure for chestnuts?"

"In two months I'll graduate from high school, class of 1975," she said. "I haven't thought much after that."

Amos nodded his head. "Well, you can teach school in McDowell County, just like your Daddy."

For sure, she could teach a few years after college before she went to graduate school. Talking to Amos, the future that had always frightened her before seemed more clear.

"Hey, Amos," Grace asked, "Did you go to school with my father?"

"Well, I'm half way between Ruby and Tom. I taught him all I knew about hunting and fishing. He couldn't teach me much book-learning, though." Amos looked ten years older than Ruby. "I skipped so much school in the spring and fall, so when I went to school in the winter, I was always in fourth grade. Your Daddy was a smart one and ambitious. He went off to war to see the world and then to college, and I barely learned to read and figure. He was smart except when he got married; begging your pardon, about your mother."

"Oh no, you're right about her," she said. They climbed steps over the stile on the Bentons' pasture fence and walked across the chicken yard into Clara's kitchen.

At lunch Grace asked Ruby, "I'd like to get my father's fiddle re-strung. Can anyone around here help me?"

"Sure," Ruby said, "Farley Dodge up the hollow can do anything with musical instruments."

Amos spoke right up with a proprietary air, "Grace, I can do that for you. I'll get strings at Miz Huffman's store."

"Settle down, Amos," Ruby spoke up, "Let Farley do what he

can do better than you. He'll fix the crack in the back too. Don't be competitive. You two are more alike than anyone around here."

"Ruby," Amos said crestfallen, "Farley's a colored man."

"He's a dark Indian with Melungeon blood," she nodded. "Why you two aren't better friends, I can't figure."

Walking back to the farm after eating Clara's homegrown lamb, peas, and potatoes for Sunday dinner, Amos angled off the path and beckoned Grace to follow him beyond the rhododendron thicket. "I'm not going the shortest route. I'm going to show you a patch of 'sang. That's what we call ginseng."

Amos bent down and pointed out a low plant that had three stalks, six inches tall, with five leaves each stalk, and a central pale-green flower.

"That's pretty hard to see unless you know what you're looking for," Grace said.

"That's the point," Amos said. "This year sang-root sells for sixty-two dollars a pound to the hardware store. They ship it to China where old men drink ginseng tea to stay young. They say in China, since the ginseng root resembles a man's body—his arms and legs; it's good for vigor."

"Can I pick some?" Grace stooped by the plant.

"No, no, pass over three plants before you pick one," Amos said. "'Sang grows scarce, like anything else, if you pick too much. You have to be patient and take only mature plants, so they grow heavy roots and put out all their seed. Wait until a plant has red berries; collect these seeds next fall, and plant them somewhere else. I spread the seeds around, in case anybody finds one patch and digs it all up."

"Is ginseng good for anything else?" Grace asked.

"Any plant is worth something just holding the dirt together." Amos smiled. "I've tended this patch since your Daddy died. Come fall I'll dig a big root and show you how it looks."

"Amos, do you eat ginseng?"

"Nah, I can't afford to. But nobody around here believes that Chinese malarkey about 'sang being a love potion, but I'm glad to

21

sell it to somebody in another country who does. Old folks around here just lose their teeth and fade off like an unstoked fire."

4

As Grace walked through the orchard to the farmhouse Sunday afternoon, in the yard below she could see her stepfather's navy-blue Pontiac Grand Prix. Tolly was leaning on the hood in his gray pinstriped suit pants. She sensed his exasperation that he had to leave his golfing weekend.

"Your mother's all upset with you, Dabney," Horace Taliaferro stammered as she approached. Everyone in Richmond called her Dabney.

"Hello, Tolly," Grace said. Tolly had been her father's first roommate at the University. That was how her parents met. Tolly introduced them when Eleanor and Tolly's sister visited Charlottesville.

"What on earth have you done?" he demanded. "All this junk was supposed to be sold yesterday." He pointed to tools piled up in the yard. "Good riddance to bad memories for your mother."

"You never told me this farm is going to be mine." Grace spread her arms around to embrace the whole valley, ridge to ridge. "You didn't ask my opinion."

"You were at school."

"Not every day for the last seven years," Grace said. "I'll decide myself what I want to do." She had never respected Tolly, who indulged her mother's vanity and spent her money.

"By your stopping the auction," Tolly said, "Ruby can't pay her hospital bills."

"I'll pay them for her; I can sell a stock," she said. "I'm going to live here with Ruby."

"There's no point, Grace Dabney," he said. "The house will be flooded next year."

"What?" She faced off her stepfather in the yard. "What did you say?"

Tolly said, "The electric-company dam will flood the whole valley."

"What do you mean? Why?"

"They need power."

"What about these fields and pastures? What about the house and the barn? The apple trees uphill and the sugar maples by the river?"

"The orchard will be lakefront, but that won't do anybody any good, because the reservoir will fill the whole valley. This road doesn't go anywhere anyway."

"What about the neighbors' farms?" Grace gestured down the road.

"Don't be sentimental, Dabney," Tolly said. "These people have not heard about the dam yet. No point in alarming them about something they can't stop."

"Where's the dam planned?"

"Down the creek, at the turn up the valley, at some churchyard."

"That's Ruby's church." Grace had never seen where her father was buried in the church graveyard. "But there's bound to be some sort of legal process before the power company can build a dam." She remembered her stepfather's law firm worked with the power company.

"This dam site has been recorded on the utility books for years," Tolly said. "The Federal Power Commission will hold hearings this summer, but they should be no obstacle because state government will support it. You're just lucky for your investment that the dam over in West Virginia was defeated, so CUPCO has to look at smaller sites like this." CUPCO was the acronym for Commonwealth Utility and Power Company.

"But come along, Dabney," Tolly said impatiently. "I have come to take you to dinner with your mother."

"Where is she?" Grace asked.

"Eleanor's too nervous to see this place again," Tolly said. "She's waiting for us at the Homestead. I've come to fetch you while she is resting." Grace knew that meant her mother was alone drinking. "I'll wait while you put on a dress," he said.

24

"You go on ahead. I'll drive over in my own car."

The Homestead was an expensive resort hotel half an hour south. When Eleanor married Tom and moved to his farm in McDowell County, she had nothing in common with Tom's country people, so she would run off on weekends to party with her Richmond friends at the Homestead. Grace had first met Tolly there. Tom hated the snobbery of the resort, its golf courses, tennis courts, indoor swimming pools, horse stables, and ski slopes.

When Grace was a little girl, she had to sit stiff and polite, dressed like a doll in clean clothes, under the yellow and white awnings that covered broad verandas while Eleanor was playing games. Eleanor even called her daughter, "Doll." When Grace was really little, she originally thought the resort's vast acres of green lawns were pastures without cows.

While her mother was cocktailing after tennis matches, Grace had wandered alone in the hotel through endless sitting rooms. All her mother had told her was, "Behave yourself." In the top drawer of an antique desk with spindly legs, she had found engraved stationery to draw on. She drew the birds that her father had showed her in the woods, until her mother found her asleep on some striped taffeta sofa.

Eleanor had started giving Grace tennis lessons when she could barely hold a racket. Eleanor played tennis, Grace thought, to wear short skirts to show off her legs, and she taught me so she could beat me.

Eating Baked Alaska after dinner that Sunday at the Homestead, Tolly told Grace, "I have arranged to sell this property to the electric company before the dam is announced. I'll invest your profit in stocks to provide income for you, so you can return to England."

You'd like that, Grace thought. She figured Tolly was happier when she was gone. Maybe this dam deal was a means for Tolly to earn some money of his own.

In a husky voice, her mother said, "Do what Tolly says is best. You don't need to worry your sweet head about finances.

Tolly always takes care of everything." Though cigarettes had taken their toll, graveling her voice and creasing her skin so beauty creams could not smooth her face, Eleanor was chic and ageless.

"But I don't want a dam here," Grace said. "I want to keep the farm."

"Nonsense, Dabney. That place is such a dump," Eleanor said. "You can travel and live with me between trips."

"Don't you see? Staying at the farm is a chance for me to get to know my father." She ran her fingers through her mop of curls. "Eleanor, Tolly, I want to be called Grace now."

5

Grace drove Ruby to the University Hospital in Charlottesville on Wednesday for the orthopedic doctor to check how her leg bone was setting. The doctor liked Ruby, although she sassed him.

"Now, Doctor Luke, it's time you take off this fool cast so I can get back to work."

"Why don't you act your age, Miss McAuley?" His tone was exasperated because he was tired, but he smiled at the old lady's nerve. "And take it easy."

"Why, if I start acting my age," Ruby said, "I might start feeling my age, and there's too much work to do on the farm."

After judging that the bone was knitting well enough, he replaced Ruby's big cast with a smaller one, so she could hobble around on crutches.

"You stay off that leg another month," Dr. Luke said, "and don't you do any heavy lifting. That's what your niece is here for. Grace, you hear?" He directed her to take all the work she could off Ruby's shoulders.

In the car on the way back to Jack Creek, Ruby outlined her plans for planting her spring garden, a month late, and for collecting her animals that were spread around the neighbors. Farmers' lives along the creek were busy, so they were glad to give back Ruby's chores they had covered while she was laid up.

Charlie Dorset brought back Ruby's big brown-and-white cow, Jers, and Ruby showed how to drain milk by pulling her hands down the smooth skin of the udder. Grace agreed to milk Jers every twelve hours, six a.m. and six p.m.

"Strip each teat good," Ruby told her. "Don't leave any milk in her."

The next morning when the alarm blared at five-fifty, Grace rolled over under the feather comforter. She always hated getting out of bed, and April before daylight in the mountains was cold.

Little warmth from the oil burner in the living room or the wood cookstove reached her upstairs bedroom.

"Rise and shine," Ruby yelled from downstairs.

Grace put on her glasses before she got out of bed, then pulled on her sweatpants from gym class over her nightgown, and stumbled downstairs in her sock-feet. Accustomed to early hours from a lifetime milking, Ruby was already in the kitchen. In the back hall Grace pulled on the man's work pants, insulated jacket, and boots.

The early morning fog misted her glasses wet. Before the sun burned off the mist, she followed fence posts, one by one. Dark posts emerged every twelve feet from the world of whiteness until she reached the barn. After she slid open the heavy wood door and closed it, she stuffed the gloves in the coat pocket and warmed her hands on the cow's broad side, gathering nerve for her job. At Jers's left flank, she sat on the tippy three-leg stool, as Ruby had shown her. Accustomed to a certain steady rhythm and pressure, Jers turned her head to watch; nevertheless, the cow was patient with her clumsiness. Grace took some assurance from the big animal's rhythmic breathing, however condescending.

After pulling the last drops from the udders and filling the big bucket, she dipped a bowl of the hot fuzzy milk for Chessie the farm cat, who caught mice in the barn. The day brightened as she walked back to the house to strain the milk and chill it to keep away any bad flavor.

From the back hall she asked Ruby, "Can't Jers get used to milking at seven a.m. and seven p.m.?" Grace felt slightly put-upon getting up so early.

Ruby laughed, "Nope. Farmers are ruled by their animals, harvests, and weather. Not the other way around. Every season we have to do what needs to be done, and there's always more to do. Might as well enjoy it since we have no choice. Be grateful to work with living things." Ruby handed her some hot coffee. "Grace, don't fight Jers; work with her. You're in this together."

"I might say the same about you and your leg," Grace teased.

She could not stay glum long around Ruby.

Ruby said, "I'll serve your breakfast when you've fed the stock." Grace turned to go out again. "Remember to cut the strings off those hay bales," Ruby warned. What Ruby wanted was to be outside working herself. "If the sheep swallow them, they'll strangle. Save the twine to use later."

Grace felt flattered to be trusted driving the tractor. She ground the gears, popped the clutch, lurked backwards into the shed, then stalled.

"Oh well," she sighed. She could not heft the hay bales, so she pushed them onto the little wagon the tractor pulled, and drove across the road. Mist from the river floated in the lower meadow. Thirty sheep and ten cows waited at the gate, while she stopped to open it. As she drove through and walked back to latch the gate, they crowded around the wagon.

Back in the tractor seat, she disengaged the brake, let out the clutch more smoothly, and lurched forward. Every twenty feet or so, she stopped, walked back and pushed off a bale. She led the animals walking slowly in a wide circle on the field until four or five crowded around each bale.

When Grace returned to the kitchen command post, Ruby had started chopping a shoulder of venison. Mason jars were scalding in boiling water on the stove. Hunters on her land gave Ruby squirrels, rabbits, and haunches of deer, which she cut up and froze. The freezer was Ruby's one concession to the modern age, along with the television and an electric range for the summer. In the winter she cooked on the woodstove that doubled as heat.

"I'm not against modern appliances," Ruby said. "I just don't think dishwashers and electric tools are worth the money or reliable." Ruby still canned a batch of everything she froze in case the electricity went out longer than a couple of days.

Ruby never indulged in conveniences like store-bought butter. As she hand-cranked the metal mill to grind half of the chopped venison for sausage, she scoffed at Grace for relying on a grocery store. Moving to the table, Ruby stuffed the ground meat into skin sleeves.

"We've got all the food in the world the Good Lord give us to grow in the garden, to pick up the hollow," Ruby explained. "Why, you must learn to make mayonnaise from scratch. Just whip up two egg yolks. Mix in oil, cayenne, salt, and vinegar. You might not think that mayonnaise turns white without milk, but it does." In Richmond, Grace never cooked, and neither did Eleanor.

As the house warmed toward noon, wasps swarmed from the eaves into the kitchen. Ruby released a wasp from the house by lifting a window screen. "I never kill a living thing unless I have to. But go fetch the brown hen from the coop. That clucker stopped laying eggs," Ruby said, "so we'll eat her. We can trade some milk for some of Esther's eggs. You eat, so you might as well know that chicken meat comes from chickens."

Laid up already for six weeks, Ruby had a long list of spring chores. Whenever Grace turned her back, Ruby started another project. From watching Ruby attack her chores, Grace could see she never let up; yet there was a rhythm, a balance to her days. Ruby alternated hard work and pleasure work, but she never loafed. Instead of rocking on the porch for a break, as Grace yearned to do, Ruby did a job to make something pretty or feed the wild creatures—deadheading zinnias or filling birdfeeders.

When the mail-lady in her truck honked, Grace walked down to the mailbox, hoping for a letter forwarded to her. She was waiting to hear from Will Parker, the guy she had dated the fall semester in England. She had not seen him since she returned to Virginia at Christmas. Grace had written Will two letters, but he had not answered. She was glad there were more than enough chores to distract her.

In the mail Ruby opened at the kitchen table was a letter from the state Methodist conference asking her to be a deaconess. "Naw," Ruby said, when she read the letter. "I don't have enough education."

"Sure you do," Grace said, but Ruby refused.

Ruby was superstitious, but she had devout faith and was the leading force in her local church. She knew the Bible backwards and forwards and believed every word. Ruby was surely country wise. She knew more than Grace could ever hope to learn about animals and plants and weather. Ruby concocted herbal tea as spring tonic. She made bread yeast from scratch by boiling potatoes. But Ruby was no deep thinker. Her only reading beside the Bible was a supermarket scandal sheet that came by mail subscription. When Ruby read about UFOs and movie stars, she would accept as fact anything in print.

"Go on, Ruby," Grace teased. "No broomstick ever attacked a housewife in a closet."

"You go ahead and read those novels of yours," Ruby came back. "My magazine stories are a lot more true than that."

Grace admired Ruby because her aunt knew so much about farming. She did watch television, though. All the time Ruby was in the house, she listened to the big console TV in the living room. Its constant chatter drove Grace crazy

"My soaps keep me company," Ruby said. "I see the characters more than I see some of my neighbors."

In the afternoon, clouds darkened the sky, and rain blew against the kitchen windows when Grace came in for supper after milking.

"Except for thawing the freezer, we live just fine without electricity when storms blow trees on the power lines," Ruby said. "In the winter it takes electric crews several days to fix the wires this far in the county. Besides, when it's dark, it's time to sleep."

Even after dark Ruby kept busy, quilting, to make something beautiful. On the kitchen table with clear plastic over the vinyl tablecloth, she layered a flowered sheet for backing, Dacron batting, and one of her pieced quilt tops. Ruby showed Grace how to stitch through at four-inch intervals, cut the string, and tie off a knot.

"I charge more for hand-sewn tops than for machine stitched," Ruby said. She sold her quilts at the craft store in Jackson, the county seat.

At nine p.m., when Grace snuggled under the goose-feather comforter on her bed, her arm and back muscles were sore from farm work. Her hands were all rough and blistered. She was too tired to read more than a page from her father's book of Coleridge and Wordsworth. No wonder farmers aren't intellectuals, she thought. Too soon the next morning, before the alarm sounded, Grace woke to Ruby's "Rise and Shine" and the sound of the river.

6

I'm short and sturdy like Ruby, Grace thought, sitting on the front porch, even though we're only half blood related. Aunt Ruby and her father had different mothers. In Grace's lap was a faded pastel calico quilt pieced in a pinwheel pattern, worn thin.

Over her shoulder, rocking, Ruby said, "My mama Annabelle Benton might have sewed these soft spring colors, or your own grandmother Maud Ross, to brighten a cold winter afternoon." Ruby darned socks as she rocked. "After Annabelle died," she said, "I tended house for my father, Jasper McAuley, from the time I was eight until I was thirteen. Then he married Maud Ross, barely ten years older than me, and they had Thomas. That's your papa."

"Ruby, why didn't you ever get married?"

"When our parents died, I stayed on the farm to take care of Tom. And then when he married Eleanor, I kept house for them, and somebody needed to take care of you. Your mother didn't stay around here much, even before she moved away for good."

Grace had few early memories. On the quilt backing were rust spots from old metal springs. Some of the stitches were tiny and disciplined; others were sloppy and inconsistent as if some child had practiced piecing. Grace sensed older quilts made by earlier generations were hidden inside.

"Ruby, I want to see the layers. May I rip this quilt apart?"

"If you do it carefully."

With a knife, Grace sliced along the frayed border and through the string knots. Ruby sent her to the kitchen drawer for a fine-point stitch-ripper to pull up a corner of the pastel pinwheels without tearing the threadbare fabric. The next layer down was a crazy quilt, remnants from old clothes turned every which way like a kaleidoscope. Thick black floss ringed every piece like lead in a stained-glass window. Mud stained the next quilt, which no one had bothered to wash before covering it.

"Who made this part?" she asked.

"I think your Daddy's paternal grandmother stitched this crazy quilt, Inge Schuster. She came over from Germany and married Angus McAuley, a Scotsman in McDowell County. Or coulda been his other grandmother Rebecca Ryan from Tidewater. Virginia's mountains were settled by Germans and Scots who wanted to keep to themselves," Ruby said. "They made little fuss about politics or wars, the Revolutionary War or the War Between the States. Presbyterians, Lutherans, and Methodists, they wanted to work hard, and in the mountains we have to."

Dictated by thrift more than design, random colors and textures were strewn around the crazy-quilt top. This layer, also worn thin, had been used for a long time and patched in places with brighter swatches. Brides, mothers, and little girls—all Grace's ancestors had lived on this land. They sewed this quilt, and it kept their families warm. She tried to imagine the lives they had led up here, so different from her life in Richmond with her mother.

To leave the quilt mostly intact, Grace turned up only a corner to see the next layer down. The bottom layer was thicker-mesh cloth, hand-woven brown and blue gingham plaid. She carefully pulled up the backing to reveal wool batting laid in rows. Not store-bought Dacron batting for warmth, but real scratchy wool.

"Straight from the sheep, washed and carded. From sheep grown on the farm," Ruby said.

Their folks had lived on this land for a long time. McAuleys had farmed Jack Creek Valley in McDowell County since the Revolutionary War. Men married women from the creek or up at the courthouse. Ignoring the Civil War, men tilled steep rocky fields and raised sheep on steeper pastures, hunted deer and chopped timber. Women gardened and cooked, washed and scrubbed, spun, wove and knit, canned and preserved, shared the men's chores, tended sick stock and the men.

Now, in the 1970s, somebody in each family worked a town job for cash, some as far away as Staunton. Lucky wives along Jack Creek drove half an hour to Jackson, thankful to work as feed-store cashiers, waitresses in the Maple Leaf restaurant, maids at the motel, or secretaries in the county courthouse. Others carpooled the 75-minute drive to sew clothes in the mills in Staunton.

Sons and daughters moved away to Staunton or Harrisonburg for factory jobs. High school graduates who did go to college did not return. Though plenty tried, a few men earned a living as car mechanics, but most farmers, except Ruby, fixed their own equipment. Fixing engines was the only thing Ruby did not keep up with herself; Waller maintained the tractor in exchange for her babysitting Loretta.

Grace had heard her stepfather's business cronies criticize hillbillies for living off welfare, but she was learning how proud these hill folk were. Ruby's neighbors along Jack Creek would not take government money no matter how sparse their harvest. In hardship they helped each other, just as they had spread around Ruby's chores when she was laid up. Or they did without. Sheer determination squeezed a living from the thin rocky mountain soil. Most of what they ate, they grew. Only on the narrow floodplain by the river was there enough fertile soil for growing hay or corn for silage. Cash crops were sheep and hogs, timber and apples. And ginseng for the few, like Amos, who still knew where to find it.

7

Every other day, Farley Dodge walked down from his hollow at the head of the creek to rub Ruby's healing leg. Farley concocted liniment from his spring water mixed with goldenseal and comfrey that Amos had picked. Farley rolled up Ruby's work pants and took off the removable splint she wore to protect her weak leg.

"Farley, you be quick now," Ruby would say. "I have chores to tend to. What business do I have sitting in the middle of the day?"

"Relax now, Ruby." Farley told stories as he massaged Ruby's calf. "Old Indians say water from this spring heals diseases. Indians would carry their sick people for miles to bathe with the waters. Folks used to say that whoever took the first drink on a Saturday morning would have a long life and would be able to tell the future; never have sickness or sorrow. Lucky me, I drink from the spring every morning."

Farley's rough hands massaged the herbal liniment into Ruby's leg. His hands were callused from working with wood. "Really, it may be the touching more than the magic juice that fixes muscles," he said. "It's the belief that the spring will cure more the water itself."

Thursday evening, her second week at the farm, Grace helped the churchwomen serve the monthly dinner for the Ruritan Club. All day in her own kitchen, despite the leg cast, Ruby baked loaves of salt-rised bread, venison meatloaf, butterscotch and lemon custard pies. She heated up homegrown green beans stewed with bacon fat, and creamed potatoes with milk. From Ruby's pantry, Grace took down jars of spicy applesauce and watermelon-rind pickles canned the previous summer. She whipped up Jers's heavy cream to top the pies and helped load Ruby's bowls, pots, and jars into the farm pickup.

Ruby hobbled out to the truck after changing from her housedress and kitchen apron into the olive-green knit pantsuit she wore to church. She had carefully slit open the pant leg along the seam to fit over her cast and rolled up the fabric above her knee, to sew again when the cast came off. Grace had washed her own bushy hair and put on a skirt instead of the jeans she wore working all week.

At the turn in the road up Jack Creek Valley, Brewers Notch Methodist Church sat on a wedge of land between the creek and the country crossroads. Five women helped carry the food from Ruby's truck into the church kitchen. Grace greeted Clara Benton who had nursed Ruby for a month, Esther Conway who traded eggs for milk, and Hilda Huffman who tended the valley store. She met Millie Dorset from two farms south and white-haired Emily Puffenbarger, the retired school librarian.

Since Ruby had prepared the food, all the others had to do was brew the coffee, set the table, and put out the serving dishes. Ruby limped, getting in the way, until Grace fetched a chair from the hall and pushed her down to sit. Grace saw nothing else she could do in the church kitchen.

"Ruby, I'll be back in a minute," she said. "Yell if you need me to help; I'm going for a walk."

Over in the grove by the church, on high ground above spring floods, were thirty small stones. Grace found her father's marker next to his father Jasper, and his two wives, Annabelle and Maud. It was a thin white stone: "Thomas Ross McAuley, 1932–1968," she read aloud, and mumbled to herself, "He was only thirty-six when he died." In 1951, when he graduated from McDowell County High School, her father had joined the army and fought in the Korean War. Then he went to the University on the GI bill, met and married her mother in Charlottesville, and they had her in 1958, just after he graduated.

Grace missed her father. She felt cheated that he left her so early. She wondered if any of his spirit lingered nearby in the quiet grove of trees.

"I'm fine, Daddy," she whispered, "you taught me how to whistle to birds, to sing, and love poetry."

From the trees Grace watched a dozen men park their pickups on the semi-circle dirt driveway off the highway. She recognized men from the auction and the store. They stood outside talking, thumbs hooked in back pockets, weight shifting foot to foot. Grace waved to Amos, who rode up with Harry Benton.

Sally Bee arrived with Waller and their daughter. Waller looked like a grown man next to Sally Bee. Except for her bulging stomach, she was a slight girl. Seeing Grace in the cemetery grove, Sally Bee walked over to talk to her, and Waller carried Loretta into the church hall.

"Ruby will watch Loretta while we talk," Sally Bee said, easing her swollen feet by sitting on the bench. "I'm glad to see you."

"Hey, how are you feeling?"

"This baby will come before it gets too hot. Next month or three weeks, who can tell?"

"Sally Bee, what does B. stand for?"

"Nobody knows. It was my grandmother's initial. We pass it on to women in our family. You know, Grace, Tim is buried in this graveyard, next to his daddy and mother."

"What happened to Tim?" Grace asked. She knew Mrs. Pollock had died in childbirth when they were kids. She could vaguely picture the figure of Waller's mother, the same narrow hips as Sally, next to her big husband with two half-grown sons, already the size of men.

"Tim died in Vietnam."

"Didn't you have a crush on Tim when we were younger?"

"Yes, I went steady with him even before high school. Our families said we were too young to get married before he went to the war."

Sitting on the grass, Grace listened to Sally Bee. "Wild-eyed as Tim was, he wouldn't have been as good a husband as Waller. When the news came about Tim, I went over to clean up for Waller and his father. Shortly after, their father died in a trucking accident. He was missing two days, and everybody was scared what

39

he had done to himself in his grief." She shifted her weight, her hands on the bench lifting and re-settling.

"What happened was—" Sally Bee said, "driving his logging truck back from the pulp mill in West Virginia, the truck went off the two-hundred-feet embankment on the Gauley River. They found him, still alive pinned under the truck. He died in the hospital from being crushed inside. First I went to comfort Mr. Pollock," Sally Bee said, "and then Waller comforted me, and we got close. I didn't want Waller to be so alone, losing all his family and all. So we got married."

Grace asked, "Sally, how can you link your fate with one person for the rest of your life?"

"Well, we both kinda just knew. We didn't so much fall in love, as fall in bed."

"Weren't you afraid he'd leave you?"

"He had no place to leave to. I was the last person alive he knew."

"Sally, you're the most alive person I know. Weren't you sorry to leave school?"

Sally shook her head. "Grace, you've got to picture what you want to happen."

Grace thought for a minute about seeing teenage mothers—in the grocery store with three kids—who didn't look as though they could read. Who really makes a good mother? she wondered. She knew Sally Bee was brimming with love.

"I don't know if I'll ever get married and have kids," Grace said. "I feel way too young to handle a relationship. When I visited Sweet Briar College, all the seniors showed off their engagement rings." She noticed Sally Bee didn't wear any diamond, just a thin gold band.

Grace started to sing, "I never will marry. I'll be no man's wife. I intend to live single the rest of my life. *Plaisir d'amour ne dure qu'un moment. Chagrin d'amour dure toute la vie.*"

"What's that mean?"

"The joys of love don't last but a moment. The pains of love

40

endure a whole life long."

"Grace, sing something you want to come true."

"So, what's it like being married?" Grace asked.

"We love each other, sure, but marriage is like a business too. We divide up responsibilities. When Waller's away at work, I run the place. But I keep quiet when Waller needs to think he's boss, say, if he's ornery from his boss yelling at him."

"I can't imagine ever marrying any of the guys I have met so far." Except Will, Grace thought, maybe Will.

In the church kitchen, the ladies had reheated the green beans on the stove and warmed the creamed potatoes in the oven. They laid out the steaming dishes in front of their husbands and neighbors on the two long tables in the hall. Grace wondered at these women, who were content at the kitchen counter while their menfolk gobbled food and gabbed pig prices in the church hall.

She had little she could share with the women about school, going to plays in London or skiing over Christmas in Switzerland, so she listened to their talk of relatives, recipes, accidents, illnesses, and expenses. Sally Bee chatted right along with the older women as one of them—farmwife and mother. Loretta darted around, and Ruby fed her mouthfuls of potatoes when she stopped still.

"Sally Bee, will you fix a plate to carry by Fred Swope's cabin?" Ruby said. "He didn't come tonight." Ruby told Grace, "Fred's a simple soul we all look after."

Ruby donated most all the food for Ruritan dinners. From her garden and mountain-hollow foraging, she could feed the whole creek community. She was by no means rich, but it was her contribution to raise money for religious education.

"Government rules aren't going to keep our schoolchildren from Bible study," Ruby said. She parked the short church bus in her yard, and before she broke her leg, one day a week she drove each grade in the elementary school a half-mile back and forth for Bible study at a church in Jackson. As soon as Grace could go to Staunton to get a bus-driver's license, she would take over the Wednesday bus driving from Millie Dorset.

41

Old men with weathered faces at the Ruritan dinner flirted and teased Grace when she pushed open the swinging kitchen door to remove empty serving bowls and dinner plates. They said, "Jess like your Daddy" again. Most had known her father and told her what a smart fellow Tommy was, going off the college and coming back a schoolteacher. Waller Pollock and two younger farmers at the Ruritan meeting—silent, stolid, and thick-bodied— wore gold wedding rings. She wondered where the single guys were.

As Grace served the pie plates and poured more coffee, she heard the men talking of the announcement that week about the dam proposed on Jack Creek. In the newspaper the electric company said the reservoir would cover mostly Forest Service land.

"It might flood some pastures, I figure," said Enoch Conway, who had no pastures, "but it will surely bring money and jobs that we need and keep our sons from moving away." Nobody at dinner knew where on Jack Creek the dam was planned, but the Ruritan men did not judge it would be up as far as Brewers Notch.

"Just not much water flow to fill a dam, I reckon," Charlie Dorset said.

"Nothing we can do to stop something the government decides to do," Aaron Miller said.

"I'm plimeblank not moving," Amos vowed. "Nobody will run me off."

"No place to move to," said Harry Benton. "Fertile land in this county is getting too scarce and too expensive for farmers to buy. Mountain ridges what we can't plow, the Forest Service already owns. The rest is getting carved into house lots."

"I ate right smart a piece of Ruby's pie; I was pie hungry." Enoch Conway said, patting his stomach, then said more seriously, "Flatlanders who come to the Sugar Festival are buying up any other land for second homes."

The County Chamber of Commerce organized spring and fall festivals to lure tourists. They swarmed the elementary school for

42

the pancake breakfast at the Maple Sugar Festival in March, and in October they crowded mountain roads to see fall colors. The tourists who bought pottery, whittling, and jams at the craft co-op in town where Ruby sold her quilts also bought prime land for summer homes or "investment."

"That real-estate fellow Kelly drives him a nice four-wheel-drive Jeep," Harry said, "and we just watch taxes go up."

"Things from the outside tend to kill us," Amos said. "Like the chestnut blight. I'd just as soon take down the bridges. Can't keep out bad air that rides down the Valley from factories up north. I hear acid rain can kill off trout in streams."

"Go on, Amos," Enoch Conway said, good-natured. Grace knew Amos did a lot more reading than he let on, but acted the clown nevertheless.

"Till now we've saved this county because nobody wanted it," Amos said.

"Soil is too thin for farming," Charlie Dorset said, "but it's good enough for sheep grazing."

Amos said, "Used to be, nobody would come up this way except sheep and Mother Earth homesteaders. Hippies, those that stayed, have turned out all right. Real good citizens, they are as tight about outsiders as we are. Close the gate at the county line, I say."

From her stepfather Grace knew that the dam was planned for right here, on top of Brewers Notch Methodist Church, at the turn up Jack Creek Valley, flooding the road that went nowhere. She listened to the men. There was no more farmland to move to in McDowell County, and land in any other nearby county was too expensive. That resort in Bath County had driven up prices. To the east, interstate cloverleafs, subdivisions, and factories were covering fertile land in the Shenandoah Valley. To the north and west was West Virginia, even rockier than McDowell.

"But the dam is right here, right on top of the church," Grace blurted out. "Our farm and yours will be flooded."

The room buzzed with the farmers' alarm. "Grace, why on

earth?" "Do you know for sure?"

She was ashamed to admit her stepfather worked for the power company. She carried thick white church dishes to the women washing plates in the double sink, rinsing them in steaming hot water, drying with white linen towels, and stacking them in white metal cabinets.

Their land would be flooded, this little valley where families had all lived for generations, intermarrying sons and daughters. The fabric of fields and fences, like a crazy quilt, was knit together by kinship and kindness. Nowhere, even if they could find land they could afford to buy, would all these farmers find land together to live again as neighbors.

8

Grace had gone back to sleep another two hours after she milked the cow Saturday morning. In her dream—the thread of fishing line rolled like a radio wavelength above the still pond until the fly dropped, just so. Again the line whipped in the air and rolled in smooth cadence to drop the fly twenty degrees to the left. Who was casting, she did not know; Grace wondered at the silence and symmetry. Then, as she saw she was casting at the edge of the pond, the line snarled, backed and kinked in the air. The kink was her fault. Contrite, she apologized to her father, who was teaching her to fly-fish.

When Grace opened her eyes and sat up to look out the window to gauge the day, she saw a two-tone green VW bus parked in the meadow by the river. When she stumbled through the kitchen, a pudgy bearded fellow was drinking coffee with Ruby.

"Grace, this here is Sam Bennett," Ruby said. "He comes up weekends to study the bugs in our river. I told him my city niece goes back to bed after the morning milking." She got a charge out of teasing her.

Grace nodded to Sam on her way through the back hall to splash her face in the bathroom. She was not ready to be noticed, so she did not look at him.

Ruby yelled through the open window on the wall between the kitchen and bathroom, "You want some trout for breakfast?"

"Sure, Ruby," Grace answered, closing the curtains tighter over the bathtub. She was embarrassed that the window was open with some guy about her age at the stove, sautéing onions and mushrooms.

When Grace came back into the kitchen, Ruby was saying from the chair, "Naw, Sam, I can't accept what you say about the ocean covering McDowell County. My Bible says nothing about rocks 500 million years old."

"Ruby, there is geological proof." From the reddish-brown

hair and beard and tendrils curling from under his green-plaid flannel shirt, Grace guessed hair grew between his toes like Tolkien's hobbits.

"We have this argument every time," Sam said. His accent was pure Georgia cracker.

"I'll stick to the Good Book, thank you," Ruby said.

"Ruby, keep seated," Sam said, as he flopped fish onto plates. "Better get waited on as long as you can. I caught those trout for breakfast in your front yard. It's much too pretty to flood."

"You know, that dam really scares me," Grace said. "I just got here, and suddenly they want to flood my Daddy's farm."

"Oh, it's no surprise. The electric company has had its eye on this valley for a long time, looking for steep slopes and sparse population. They're denied a dam site one place and propose another right away."

"What do you know, Sam, about this dam on Jack Creek?" Ruby asked.

"The proposed depth will come right about up to the roof of your barn," he said. "That means water level 150 feet up the slope from the house."

"How do I find out more about the dam?" Grace asked.

"Go to Richmond to check the plans. Utility records are public information," Sam said, "if you ask the right way. And you're more clean-cut than I am."

After they finished the fish, Ruby said, "Sam, why don't you take Grace down to the river and show her the bugs you're collecting?"

"Sure, glad to recruit a field assistant."

She followed Sam out the back hall. He was short, about 5' 6", hardly taller than she was. Initially, she thought the guy looked inconsequential, but welcomed a break from chores. He was not exactly fat, but his beard was so fuzzy he looked round.

In his lime-and-olive VW bus parked by the river, Sam showed her racks of glass bottles where he stored the insects. "These are stonefly and mayfly nymphs I found in the riffles this morning, and caddisfly larvae will be ready to hatch first of the month."

Grace could see subtle distinctions between the legs and body length of different species. "What's the point of catching bugs?" she asked.

"Different insects can survive in different levels of pollution, so they're a biological index of stream health." Sam picked up a bottle with a mayfly floating in liquid. "Your clean river is my baseline to compare to other rivers that have too much junk in them like silt, fertilizers, and pesticides from plowed fields, or too many nutrients from feedlots and sewage-treatment plants, or heavy metals from parking lots and industry outfalls."

"Sheep and cows wade in Jack Creek," Grace said.

"Oh, the creek's not pristine right here with the cows," Sam said, "but it sure is cleaner than downstream. I record gradients of pollution from the spring up Ruby's hollow, pastures along Jack Creek, to yucky pulp mills on Jackson River in Covington, shopping malls along the James River, all the way to the oil refineries on Hampton Roads. Jack Creek is the cleanest place in the state because there is no industry upstream."

"That's a lot of traveling," she said. "My mother lives by the James River in Richmond. Sam, do you live in this bus?" Wooden shelves held cooking pots and books. "Looks like you have a kitchen and library."

"And my rolling laboratory, too," he said. "I have simple tastes. Oh, I like luxury, all right. Green grass and burbling brook is better than parking on pavement, or my basement in Charlottesville."

"Sam, really, is there any way to stop the dam?"

"Well, sure, organize folks along the creek to call their legislators," he said. "But my bet is that these country people want nothing to do with government, even to protect their own interests. If anybody can, maybe you can convince your neighbors, since you're one of them."

Sam intrigued Grace. He did not flirt with her, but with Ruby.

He did not look as good as Will in England, but he was not a peacock like Jared. While she watched, he rolled up his sleeping bag in the back of his bus, stowed the foam pad under his shelves, and pulled plywood doors over his racks of glass jars, ready for rough roads.

"Well, I've got to take off," Sam said. "I have two days' driving to field sites before class on Monday."

"What are you studying?" Grace asked.

"Ecology at UVa," he said. "I'm almost a junior, half way through my degree in Environmental Sciences. Hey, take care of Ruby, will you? She's something special."

Grace stepped back to wave goodbye. She was sorry to see someone closer to her age leave the valley. Everyone else on the creek was over forty. Now that Sally Bee was married with a daughter and another baby on the way, she was as good as thirty.

"Will you open gates for me?" Sam asked, leaning out his window. Grace ran ahead of the bus, opened and closed two sets of pasture gates.

At the road he said, "Good luck with Jers." Grace knew Ruby had been telling stories on her attempts at milking.

"When will you be back?" she asked.

"Oh, a week or two." Teasing from Ruby and Sam was a form of affection, and they all wanted her to loosen up.

That week after milking and feeding the stock, Grace practiced driving the school bus, dug a waterbar across the driveway, and painted the gas tank red. She read poems by Wordsworth and Coleridge in her father's books. *The child is father to the man. The world is too much with us.* To graduate from high school, she had to mail a term paper within a month.

Grace found Amos wading through a rhododendron thicket where the sun hit the hillside. Come first of June, the blossoms would cover the slope in pink.

"Amos," she said, "maybe the people who live along Jack Creek can stop the dam."

"Not likely. You can't fight both government and the power

48

company in cahoots," Amos said, "and I plimeblank ain't moving. I reckon I'll have to reverse evolution and learn to breathe underwater."

She tripped over an exposed root on the path and recovered her footing.

"Grace, you move like one of those ice skaters on TV. They come so close to catastrophe, crossing their skates, and never do," Amos said. "Gracie, you're never gonna see many critters if you crash like a bulldozer."

Grace thought her name was so inappropriate. She had little luck dating in Richmond; she felt graceless around guys. Just because their mothers were friends, Kenneth had driven her to a Christmas party in ninth grade. She had told Eleanor that Kenneth was cute and then heard her mother on the phone telling his mother that little Dabney had a crush on him. After that, she never again trusted Eleanor with a confidence.

"Amos, I'm hopeless," Grace said. "I don't see how I can ever walk without making noise."

"Sure you can. Walk like an Indian," Amos answered. "Come down first on your heel and then roll the ball of your foot."

As she tried, leaves crackled under her feet.

"You gotta look where you're stepping too." Amos chuckled.

"How can I look at my feet, Amos, if I'm looking at the flowers and birds?"

"Well, you can see it all if you don't move so fast. It does no harm to keep an eye out for rattlers, either. They're waking up this time of year."

"Snakes? Jeez, Amos, I'm not coming up the hollow if I'm going to get bitten by a poisonous snake."

"Not all snakes are poisonous. Besides, no snake wants to bother you, if you don't step on it," Amos said. "Takes 'em energy to manufacture poison, which they'd waste, 'cause they can't eat you; you're bigger than a mouse. Try walking quiet again, if you want to stalk. I ain't your Daddy, but I aim to show you things he would have."

49

That week, near the end of April on an overcast day, a forcibly-folksy man who worked for the power company paid calls on the landowners along Jack Creek, knocking on doors and drinking coffee at kitchen tables. James Bates was fat like a watermelon and pale pink like watermelon-rind, as if he had never seen the sun.

"Miz McAuley, we're prepared to offer you a generous price for your land. We'll pay you the official appraisal plus a fifteen-percent bonus, if you sign this week," Bates said, waving his coffee cup without drinking or spilling any. "Go ahead and think about it all night if you wish."

While Bates addressed his persuasion to Ruby, Grace cut around brown spots in cooking apples stored in the root cellar since November. Ruby went on mixing flour, ice water, and lard for pie dough, rolled out two circles on the marble slab, flopped the crusts in two glass pie plates, filled them with apples Grace had diced, spread around pats of butter, sprinkled cinnamon and sugar, and formed lattice crusts.

"We will provide real-estate counselors to help you relocate wherever you wish," he said, lisping slightly. Grace guessed Bates was an overgrown mama's boy who got this job through family connections. She did not warm to his innuendo that he was doing them a favor.

The phone rang and startled James Bates. Grace picked up. It was Sally Bee, asking if she could drop off Loretta while she went to the baby-doctor's office in Staunton.

"Sure, Sally Bee," Grace said. "Do you want me to drive you?"

"No, I'm fine. You can chase Loretta for Ruby."

"Well, Miz McAuley," Bates said to Ruby, "sign here to accept our generous offer." He had a form right then, right there.

"No, sir, Mr. Bates," Grace said. He had been ignoring her as if she were a child. "We don't need to think it over. We won't be selling our farm."

Bates turned from her to Ruby, "Miz McAuley?"

"Don't ask *me*," she replied. "*That* Miss McAuley owns the land."

When Grace went by the Conways' place to trade milk for eggs, she asked what they thought of the dam. Esther said, "We'll buy us a split-level in one of those new subdivisions in Staunton near our grandchildren."

When Grace talked to the Dorsets at the next farm down the valley, Millie said, "Charlie can move his woodworking shop anywhere." He had lamed his leg in a logging accident twenty years earlier.

She visited the other families along Jack Creek to ask them not to sign, to wait a day or a week. Esther and Enoch Conway were resigned to selling out, as well as the Dorsets and Huffmans and Breedloves. Grace was demoralized that she couldn't get any interest from her neighbors to oppose the dam.

She walked up the hollow, stepped around a rattler basking on the path, lay on a bed of moss, and looked up at the green leaves above her, rustling in the sunlight.

9

"We can't let this dam happen," said Todd Rawlings, director of a national river-conservation group. Sam had called Grace to come to the meeting of concerned citizens at the Charlottesville public library.

"We can't hope to beat them, but we can throw obstacles in their path," said Todd. "The longer we delay them, the more the project will cost, and it will become less attractive for investors than other sites." Small and balding at thirty, he was an efficient outdoorsy bureaucrat, who spent more time in the halls of Congress than paddling the rivers he loved.

"You all will have to take the lead," Todd told them. "This project on Jack Creek is small potatoes. I'm busy fighting the oil refinery proposed where the Elizabeth River enters the James River, at the other end of the state."

"We can't get anyone in state government to help us," said Gladys Conner. "The state wants to tax the power company's capital investment." Stump-shouldered, salt-and-pepper-haired, Gladys was the volunteer secretary of the state conservation association. She had the tired, sour air of fighting and losing battles without getting her expenses reimbursed.

"The Federal Power Commission has to prepare an Environmental Impact Statement before they license any hydroelectric dam," said Emma Coleman. "Our objective is to prepare questions for the scoping hearing in the EIS process. We have to do our homework so FPC does its homework."

Grace listened to learn from the older women's lobbying experience. Emma had retired to Charlottesville from the national office of the League of Women Voters. Grace had heard from Sam that Emma was fighting cancer without chemotherapy. A frail older woman, gentle and assertive at the same time, she exuded a joyous resilience.

"If you advise the strategy, Emma," Sam said, "I can help

with facts, and Grace can do footwork."

"Brilliant," Emma replied. "How much land will be flooded?"

"Five thousand acres—three thousand of National Forest and two thousand acres of private farms," he answered. "Three bridges, seventeen miles of road, thirteen families, a post office in a general store, a church with a graveyard."

"The first argument we can use is that the cost/benefit ratio is greater than one," Todd said. "That is, the costs of losing existing resources outweigh the benefits of building the dam. Benefits they claim for pumped-storage dams are peak-demand power generation and flood control downstream. Recreation is no benefit because the upper impoundment will have a drawdown of thirty feet, and the lower water level will vary ten feet. Muddy slopes will have to be fenced off. No dam out west is old enough to know the useful lifetime of such reservoirs. But all dams silt in at the tributaries and lose their holding capacity. In forty or fifty years, these reservoirs will be sand flats."

"What resources will be lost?" Emma asked.

"We have to stress economic values," Todd said. "Any industries that will be flooded?"

"Nothing. Jack Creek Valley is in a rural county," Sam said.

"If the dam is built," Emma asked, "what will the community have to pay because of lost roads? Will a school bus have to travel farther?"

"If the dam closes the road up the valley, then unflooded property will lose access," he said. "At the head of the valley, Farley Dodge's place has a dirt track that connects to Route 250. It is impassable in winter or after a rain."

"Will the higher tax base pay for cost increases?" Dennis Schaeffer asked. He was a lanky, gold-bearded physics professor at Madison College in Harrisonburg. "The state would have to replace or upgrade roads. The county has to pay for more fire and police protection, and for outside workers' kids to go to school."

"How many new jobs will there really be?" Todd asked. "Locals support projects like dams, hoping for employment, but they're deceived. Construction crews and skilled operators are imported union laborers. What else can we argue has value?"

"Well, Charlie Dorset has a carpentry shop," Grace said. "Farley Dodge makes musical instruments. He won't be flooded out, but he'll lose road access."

"On the flooded farms, what's the annual income from farming and forestry?" asked Dennis.

"You mean how many animals do we sell? Ruby sells or barters ten lambs a year and three calves."

"Multiply hers by eight or ten other farms," said Sam.

"We lease a field to Creed Huffman," Grace said. "We feed his hay to our stock; Waller Pollock keeps our tractor running; we trade the Conways milk or sausage for eggs. Ruby sells her maple syrup and quilts. Our orchard doesn't produce for profit anymore."

"But how much does Aunt Ruby earn a year from syrup and quilts? Or Charlie's Windsor chairs, or Farley's guitars? Not enough to pay the heat bill, I fear?" Emma asked.

"Ruby burns wood," Grace noted, "which she chops, and there's a kerosene burner."

"Jack Creek sounds like subsistence farming," Dennis said.

"Most families have someone working a job in town to pay for taxes," Sam added.

"What are the resources on the Forest Service land?" Gladys asked.

"Camping, hunting, some hiking and four-wheel trails," he said. "No picnic areas or shelters. A stand of virgin hemlock. The woods host wildflowers, but no known rare plants. No wetlands. Springs for water supply, but I wouldn't think there'd be enough water for two lakes."

"The geology along Jack Creek is really interesting," said Dennis. "Looking at the 1963 map, this valley offers the most different rock types in the most narrow cross section in the state. In less than a mile, ridge to ridge, are twelve layers of geologic ages, from 500 million to 350 million years old. Marine fossils are abundant on the ridge east of the valley."

"That argument won't hold much water, Dennis, to stop a dam," Gladys said. "Interesting old rocks and fossils."

"Limestone topography won't hold much water either, if the reservoir leaks into underground caverns," Dennis punned, grinning while others grimaced.

"Limestone streams in the forest have native brook trout populations. By the diversity of insect species, Jack Creek has the highest water-quality index in state surveys," Sam said. "Lots of oxygen means aquatic insects. A sluggish, stratified reservoir has fewer and less valuable species. You trade trout in the river for bass and bluegill in a lake."

"McDowell County would lose tourist dollars in trout fishing," Dennis said. "Or let's attack flawed engineering. Jack Creek does not drop far enough to provide sufficient head to produce power."

"The mountain does have a steep drop, but there may not be enough water flow to fill the upper reservoir," Sam suggested.

"The utility will press for a rush job," said Gladys. "FPC may try to adapt the EIS from the dam in West Virginia."

"If citizens bring a lawsuit, we can force delay," Todd said.

"On what basis?" Emma asked. "We must prove irreversible damage to irreplaceable resources. Anything people can do on Jack Creek better than any other place?"

"Quality of life," Grace answered. "We live next to neighbors on land owned for generations by our families."

"Can we protect the rights of the people in Jack Creek Valley to keep their lifestyle; the rights of the ecosystem to remain intact?" Dennis said.

"What about the endangered species act to protect habitat?" Emma asked. "Congress strengthened the act two years ago, and there's been no decision yet on the snail darter."

"An endangered species might be the way to go," Sam said. "We have examined only ten percent of existing species on the earth, and of those, fifty percent benefit humans pharmaceutically."

"It's too bad we can't think that species have their own right to live," Emma said, "instead of benefiting us."

"If a species' population is so reduced to be endangered," Dennis said, "then it will probably lose enough genetic diversity so it will die soon anyway. Why do we stop building a dam or chopping a forest for a dying species? Why not just say 'save the forest,' 'preserve the river'?"

"We need to protect diversity of species," Sam said. "Not individual species, but habitats where communities live. For human ecology, Jack Creek Valley or McDowell County aren't healthy because young people leave home to find work."

"How about aesthetics?" Grace asked. "The creek looks so pretty, Ruby would say because God made it that way."

"No, we've got to prove it on economics," said Gladys. "But nobody earns or spends any money."

"The rights of species and quality of life are legally defensible if we could get Jack Creek declared a scenic river," Todd said. "Then they couldn't dam it."

"It certainly qualifies," Emma said. "The criteria for scenic include fish and wildlife, geological, historical, cultural resources, no pollution, no other dams."

Todd said, "The state can declare a scenic stream and pass its own management plan that would forbid any future dams. All right, Gladys, contact the local Congressman and state representatives. Dennis, ask the state fish and game department to write a management plan."

"Riparian landowners would have to agree," said Dennis. "Would they accept restrictions, Grace?"

"What does scenic status mean?" she asked.

"Existing uses can continue, like grazing pastures and cornfields," Todd said, "but you can't build any more buildings within so many feet of the river; no subdividing land for a son to build a house. People along the river have to give conservation easements that may reduce the resale value of the land."

"Ruby and I'd be willing to do that," Grace said, "with the land we own."

"Mountain people don't cotton to having any outsiders tell them what to do," Sam said.

"That's right," said Dennis. "I attended wilderness hearings for Laurel Cliff, eight thousand acres of National Forest land in the northwest corner of McDowell County, absolutely the most wild, inaccessible tract of land in the eastern forests. That was the first time the Forest Service had ever held public hearings for wilderness, and it was a fiasco."

"What happened?" Sam asked.

"Basically, people in McDowell County said they wanted no government agency or outside agitators telling them how to manage their land," Dennis answered. "They said, 'we want to keep it to be the way it's always been.'"

"Which is exactly what wilderness designation protects, isn't it?" Emma commented. "Leave it alone."

"A local person is necessary," Todd said, "to develop local trust."

"That's where you can help, Grace. Can you organize the community?" asked Emma.

"Who will listen to me, a teenage girl?" Grace asked. Grace feared these experienced environmentalists expected too much of her, working alone in McDowell County.

"We don't expect you to do it all yourself," Emma said. "But you can do what none of us can; you were born there, and your father. Your neighbors will trust you."

"So what do I say?" Grace fussed. "I've asked them not to sell their land, and I did not convince anyone. One family has already signed the sell-agreement, but there are delays because the power company has to search title. Some of the deeds are old, handwritten."

"Get the media on the creek," Emma suggested. "Send letters to the editor of the Richmond newspaper. Get coverage on local TV; that would be Staunton. Get state-wide publicity so that legislators from Hampton Roads and Northern Virginia will hear of Jack Creek."

10

Grace was ready for a pep talk, the following Friday in early May, when she saw the green bus in the meadow by the creek. While Sam was wading upstream, collecting insects up the river, she sat on a rock by the riverbank. The breeze lifted lime-green leaves on the hill and made waves in fresh hay-grass in the pasture.

Between milking and lightening Ruby's other chores, Grace did too little sitting. Expecting Sam to appear was pleasant—just being there, warming up the rock, and listening to the wind and the riffles. After a while he came wading down the edge of the river, rubber boots to his thighs and his backpack clinking with glass bottles.

"I'm going to find an endangered species," he shouted. "That's how I can stop the dam."

"Great, but what? There are no dinosaurs here." She laughed, glad to see him, wet and scruffy in a forest-green chamois shirt, camouflage under the canopy of leaves arching above.

"Oh, I'll find a new insect, some rare freshwater mussel, or relict fish left here thousands of years ago when the river bed changed directions," Sam said.

Grace changed her tone. "Sam, the neighbors are more or less resigned to selling out, except Amos. I need to do some legal research about land condemnation and appeals."

"First thing you should do is see the creek you want to protect. How about a boat ride?" he asked. "Mighty pretty day. Floating a river is the best way to learn about where you live."

Shafts of light breaking through the branches ignited tufts of water over rocks, here and there, so that the water appeared to flicker ablaze.

"Isn't the river dangerous?" Grace asked.

"Only if it's flooding," Sam said. "We're almost in a drought now."

"I'd better not," she said.

"Shucks, leave your chores," he said. "The Tao said . . . ."

She interrupted him. "My father drowned in the river."

"Yeah, I'm sorry. Ruby told me." He sat down on the riverbank beside her rock.

"He died seven years ago," Grace said. "I'm back here for the first time since I was ten."

He said, "We won't run the whitewater below Brewers Notch. We'll put in at Conway's Ford up the road and take out at the church."

"All right, I'll pack a picnic," she said, hopping up to run to the house.

Grace and Sam both drove to the church parking lot and left her car by the river where they would take out. When she hopped in his bus, he pointed at the tallest beech in the graveyard.

"The impoundment's gonna be deeper than that tree," he said. Grace did not want water to cover her father's grave.

The bridge and the road up Jack Creek Valley would be flooded. Only at the head of the valley would the dirt track by Farley's place over the mountain to Route 250 still be above water. As Sam was untying the canoe from the roof rack, Grace asked if she could help him carry it.

"No, thanks," he said, "it's easier by myself."

Although he was short, Sam was strong. He swung the boat to his shoulders, carried it down the hill, and flipped it as he lowered it in the shallows. Grace carried paddles, lifejackets, picnic, and his fishing gear.

"Hold on to both gunnels as you step in," Sam said. "Keep your weight low and centered. The water level is so low that the creek is a rock garden."

He pushed the canoe away from shore and waded midstream before he stepped into the stern. Grace sat still as she could until she trusted the stability of the boat.

"The river has been here longer than any people, longer than the hills too," Sam said. "This valley is interesting geomorphology.

Curving rivers like the Jack are usually on flat ground. The bends along Jack Creek happened long ago when this land was meadow, before the mountains pushed up around the river."

As he steered the canoe on the placid stretch, Grace started to relax and look around as they passed woods and pastures.

"Mountains grew later," he said. "The mountains to the north rose up and cut Jack Creek off from the Potomac River drainage and connected it to the James River. So maybe there are species in here left from the Potomac River system. That's my scientific hypothesis."

Grace closed her eyes for a minute and listened. She said, "The noise of the river has so much color."

The water was so clear and the cobble bottom looked so close that the canoe appeared to float on ether. As Grace peered over the side, she saw the reflection of her face on the surface, and at the same time saw her shadow on the sand and rocks on the bottom. Circular vortex patterns printed on the surface as the water conformed to rocks, and the shadows of vortices passed over the sand.

"I can figure where the rocks are under water by reading the patterns on the surface," she said.

"That's the skill you need for reading whitewater," Sam said.

Flowing water sifted rocks according to size—pebbles, stones, and boulders. When the river flooded, it pushed around two-ton boulders like pebbles. A few freshly fractured rocks had jagged edges sharp enough to slice open a canoe. Older rocks smoothed round by eons of water littered the riverbed. Softer rocks had water-eroded pockmarks. The water rushed and swooshed downstream, conforming to obstacles in tufts of frothy water.

He said, "The Tao says water fits the form we put it in. Water is flexible and peaceable until we disturb it."

A great slab of gray stone angled from the hillside into the water.

"You can see the different colored stripes," he pointed at the cliff, "where these rocks were laid down in layers, then tilted. This valley is quartzite overlain by green shale and sandstone. Different colors indicate different periods. Dennis told us this valley has twelve geologic ages within about a mile."

"But Ruby doesn't believe your geologic history?"

"She believes her Bible more than what I can show her," Sam said. "The rocks in the valley are anywhere from 250 to 500 million years old. The eastern ridges, mostly steep cliff to the summit, are sandstone, 400 million years old, full of marine fossils. The western ridge is limestone, layers eroded and deposited, 440 to 500 million years old."

"Too long ago for me to fathom," Grace said. She trailed her hand in the water. It was still really cold in May.

"In a warm period, 500 million years ago," he said, "an ancient shallow sea lapped over the land here, so there are marine fossils on the cliff. I find scallop shells and marine critters along here imbedded in the rocks."

The river was a tunnel through green overhanging branches, with the cliff on the left. Limestone and slate formed a solid rock bottom here. Sliding over ledges into deeper water, the canoe distorted the reflection of juniper and mountain laurel on the still surface.

"Oh look, a kingfisher," Grace said. "Kingfishers were my Daddy's favorite bird—the cocky bird with the pointed head."

The blue-gray bird was a foot long, with slate-blue and chestnut stripes on her white breast, a tufted crest and long black beak. She flew inches above the riffles, following the channel, and lighted on an overhanging limb where she could scout for fish to dive-bomb. As their canoe approached in the current, the bird scolded them for encroaching—*chitter, chitter*—like a tiny automatic rattle.

"You know, the kingfisher is a symbol of life," Grace said. "In the Fisher King myth: When the king is sick, the fields in the kingdom are barren; when the king recuperates, the land is fertile again. Only fishing can restore the king's health."

The kingfisher flew low and fast above the water, away from them, *chitter-chittering*, along the opposite bank.

"The water striders are playing water polo." She pointed to inch-long bugs with long legs splayed out walking on top of the water. The slick water was smooth like glass. "Look at the flowers growing in the crack in the cliff; let's go see."

Sam angled his paddle blade to steer the boat right under the cliff. Where the river had carved a deep channel as it curved, the water was black, deep, and swift. He put his palms on the vertical rock to steady the canoe in the current, so Grace could look at the yellow flower.

"I'll have to ask Amos. He has field-guide books," she said. Out of the sun in the shadow of the cliff, she shivered.

"Remember this deep, shady hole for swimming in August," he said.

The creek stretched straight ahead for two hundred yards.

"Floating Jack Creek is an adventure like Huck Finn's," Grace said. "There's no telling what surprise is around the bend." She picked up the paddle at her feet and stuck it in the water, singing tentatively, "My life flows on in endless song." She stopped. "My Daddy used to sing that."

Grace sang out in a clear voice, resonant in the canyon of trees and rocks,

My life flows on in endless song
Above earth's lamentation.
I hear the real though far-off hymn
That hails a new creation.
Through all the tumult and the strife
I hear the music ringing.
It sounds an echo in my soul.
How can I keep from singing?

"That's an old Quaker hymn," Sam said. "I go to Quaker Meeting in Charlottesville. Grace, tell me about your father."

She was quiet for a minute remembering her father's word

63

games: "Who dat?" he would ask outside her bedroom door. And she was supposed to say, "Who dat say who dat?" And he would answer, "Who dat say who dat say who dat?" He would come in and gather her in his arms.

"He made up poems about hoot-owls and jump-frogs and bobcats." She hummed a tune from deep in her past.

"What did he do for a living up here?" Sam asked.

"He taught school and wrote poems. I reckon Ruby tended the farm then as she does now."

"What did he do with free time?"

"Oh, my Daddy knew about birds and flowers and stars. He loved his land and the woods."

"And the river?" he asked.

"Oh, the river best of all." Grace said. "We'd sit still and quiet on a swinging bridge to an abandoned cabin and watch otters play." She paused. "Sam, tell me about your family."

"There's only my father left. My mother died four years ago, after your father. I haven't seen him much since we argued about Vietnam."

"Where did you grow up?" she asked.

"In Augusta, Georgia." he said. "My father still lives in the old house that used to be country, but is now swallowed by suburbs. He doesn't talk to any of his neighbors. He worked for thirty years as a printer for the newspaper until a computer laid him off. He hates the machines that displaced him. I gave up arguing with him." Sam sounded even more southern when he talked about Georgia.

Grace didn't think that Eleanor would approve of his background.

After a while, floating down the river in silence, he said, "Feather your paddle. Turn it sideways to cut wind resistance."

"There's no wind," she said.

"You feel the difference when you paddle eight hours."

The light broke through the trees over the ridge into the cove, backlighting a spider web otherwise too fine to see.

"Sam, how can a spider throw his web all the way across the river?" she asked.

"Her web," he said. "She-spiders spin threads and hitch rides on the wind currents."

Grace was quiet until she began another song.

The water is wide, I cannot cross over.

And neither have I wings to fly.

Build me a boat that will carry two.

And both shall row, my love and I.

O love is gentle, love is kind.

Bright as a jewel when first it's new.

But love grows old and waxes cold

And fades away like the morning dew.

"You have a pretty voice," he said. "But you sing sad songs."

Grace wondered if Sam was a guy friend or could be a boyfriend. In high school she had waited for a sweetheart to pick her, but did not notice any guys who might have liked her.

"Here are the bow strokes for maneuvering in whitewater," he said.

"You said there was no whitewater," she fussed.

"Not much. 'Draw' means put your paddle in sideways, parallel to the keel, and pull it straight to the boat. Don't pull in too close or you could tip us. 'Push away' is just the opposite. Put your paddle in next to the boat and push away."

"Why tell me all this now?"

"You can't make a mistake in the bow I can't correct in the stern. If the boat starts to swamp, lean away. If you ever fall in, float upstream of the boat, feet first. Don't ever get caught between the boat and a rock. Remember the Tao: don't fight against the current, flow with it."

"Oh yeah, do you know much Chinese philosophy?" Grace asked.

"I had plenty of time to read during the war."

"Did you fight in Vietnam?"

"No, I don't believe in killing," Sam said.

"Okay, tell me more about water as the symbol of life," she said.

"The Tao says water adapts to the channel, flows fast where it's shallow and slow where it's deep. Water is humble—it flows downhill, seeking the lowest position. Water smooths over rough edges. Water is clear if you leave it alone; meddling muddies it. Like you, Grace, you calm down when you sit still."

Ahead, she heard water rushing through the rocks and felt panicky. "Sam, that rapid up ahead sounds like a freight train."

"Isn't that a beautiful sound? Have you heard the canoeists' riddle? Why is the Corps of Engineers like beavers?"

"I dunno."

"They build dams to stop the sound of running water."

"Sam, up ahead sounds rough."

"Relax; it's just a riffle, but you can learn good habits. You know, when somebody played a recording of running water, the beavers kept building their lodge higher and higher even though the water had stopped flowing."

As the force of the river pushed the canoe down the chute between the rocks, she jabbed her paddle at the water. Sam's paddle steered them through without scraping the rocks in the narrow passage. It was exhilarating.

Grace turned around to look at him. "That's terrific," she said.

Sam smiled. "Don't admire a rapid until you're past the eddy. Most times you flip, it's when you think you're through and you're not."

Ahead she heard more rapids, and she tensed again.

"These riffles are all class 1 or 2," he said. "That refers to the vertical drop. Class 4, like on the river below the church, is as difficult as I want to paddle in an open boat. Stand up and scout this rapid for us."

"Won't I tip the boat?"

"I'll hold it steady; just don't hop around." Grace stood with shaky knees.

"I can't tell which way to go. There are too many rocks." She sat on the seat with a thump and laughed. The river kept pushing them forward, so she made a quick decision. "That way, go left."

Sam let her do all the paddling. They washed through on the left and rammed a rock. He jumped out quickly, pushed off, and jumped back in.

"Turn around; look now," he said.

"This is wonderful. I want more rapids."

"Don't paddle; just float now or the trip will go by too fast," he said. "No point rushing. Let's pull into an eddy for a while."

He turned the boat upstream and edged the bow in the slack water under an old swinging bridge with no slats across the wires. She turned around so she leaned against the bow seat, facing backward.

"This river reminds of a tale," Sam started. "Once an adventurer on a long journey followed a river to a beautiful fertile valley—with refreshing waterfalls, exotic fruits and flowers, resplendent birds. So others could find the way back to this lovely land, she drew a map and presented it to her own villagers when she returned home. The wise leaders framed the map to protect it and placed it in the museum for safekeeping. Over the years the map became a treasure, as a piece of art; no one thought to follow its directions to the wilderness."

Grace opened her picnic bag and handed Sam a venison-meatloaf sandwich, with mayonnaise she had made herself, on Ruby's homemade bread.

"My mother, much as she loved me," he said, while eating his sandwich, "preferred me to stay home instead of exploring. I must go see for myself. I call it 'groundtruthing' like the term surveyors use for on-site verification. Old maps and charts may show the river bends here or there, but floods change channels. With hurricanes, ocean shorelines advance and recede. Aerial photographs may show four trees in a certain spatial relation. But the mapmaker should go to the field to confirm."

67

Grace figured the flowing river made Sam talk more than on land.

"As a scientist," he said, "I seek answers to my questions outside, paddling the river to study the river, catching fish to study fish. Hypothesis: bet some big old trout lives in that dark hole. I better fish for a while."

By the rock that formed the eddy where the canoe lodged was a deep pool of still water. Overhanging hemlock and rhododendron provided shade where trout could hide from midday sun.

Sam assembled the two halves of his fishing rod, threaded line, and tied on a fly. "Supposed to look like the insects flying around that the trout want to eat," he said.

Standing in the shallows, he cast upstream to the dark water at the edge of the pool. The fly drifted on the water, weightless, apparently unconnected to the fishing line. Sam moved the supple rod, so that the fly jumped and skipped a yard upstream. He twitched the line, pulling loops of line with his left hand.

Suddenly, a fish grabbed the fly, darted under, and the rod bent. Sam cranked the looped line to the reel, so the weight of the fish pulled some line off the reel. The fish did not budge, and he waited, keeping tension on his line and his rod tip up. Then the good fish surfaced, jumped, and ran. As he gave it line, the reel ratchet whined; he took it up and cranked in. Soon, he pulled the fish over to his feet, reached down, wet his hands, and held up a fourteen-inch silver fish with rosy spots.

"Rainbow trout," Sam said. He slipped the hook from the trout's lip to release it.

"Like a butterfly in the water," Grace said.

He cradled the fish gently, steady in the water, so oxygen in the river flowed over its gills, then its tail flicked, and it flashed away.

"Daddy used to fish and tie flies to sell up at the store."

"I would have liked your father," Sam said. "Anything else to eat?"

Grace tossed him a banana. She drank more water from the Ball jar she'd filled.

Into a limestone-rock ledge where they stopped, water had bored a cylindrical hole five inches deep, still filled with water although the river level was lower. At the bottom Grace could see some color. First she thought it was a mussel shell. She could fit just one finger in. She pulled out a pottery shard, etched with purple on both sides.

"Sam, this is from an old teacup," she exclaimed. "It could be my ancestors', a hundred, two hundred years old. This piece of history seems older than your 500-million-year-old rocks." She zipped the shard into her jacket pocket for safekeeping.

"How about more river songs?" he asked leaning back, peeling his banana.

"You sing," she said.

So Sam tried, off-key: "I've got peace like a river, I've got peace like a river, I've got peace like a river in my soul." He stopped singing and put the banana peel back in the picnic bag.

She said, "Virginia has so many river songs:"

O Shenandoah, I long to see you.

Far away you rolling river.

O Shenandoah, I long to see you.

Away, I'm bound away, across the wide Missouri.

"Sam," she interrupted her song. "I can't find anybody around here who wants to do anything to save this river."

"Well, you're not an outsider. You should have a better chance talking to country folk than bearded professor types like Dennis," he said. "If anybody can convince them, you can."

"I'm not having any luck," she said.

"Or determination. You want to be a writer; write letters to state newspapers. Get county schoolkids to write letters to legislators, to the governor. School's still in session another two weeks. Look," he said. "Maybe that's what you've come home to do."

"Oh, look at the otter slides, hey look," she said, pointing at the slick mud chutes, "on the riverbank under the bridge where I used to sit with my father." She bounced and leaned over the left side of the canoe.

"Sam, what do you want to be reincarnated as?" she asked.

"Beg pardon?" he said.

"Come back as in your next life?" She said with emphasis, "I'd be an otter, playing all the time."

"You'd better save the otters' river in this life," Sam said, "if you want to be one, or they'll be endangered."

She asked again, "How about you?"

He stretched his arms wide, encompassing the sky and trees and water. "Reincarnation? I'll be October. I'd like to come back every year as October."

"Wow," she paused. "I never thought of a month." From Sam she could learn a better way of seeing the world. "How about soul," she asked, "do you believe we have souls?"

"Well, the Welsh believe each piece of water, each lake and river, has a spirit in it. So I guess my soul will rest in the water somewhere, or everywhere. I'll be comfortable if my soul is part of a flowing river, or still water like the Twenty-third Psalm. But not a dam impoundment." And they were silent until they reached the takeout by the church at Brewers Notch.

With the canoe on his shoulders, Sam cautioned, when they were walking up the path, "You may want to watch out for poison ivy: three leaves." He stored the canoe behind the church; he'd load it on his bus later.

He picked some green leaves and told her to mash the juice on her legs and arms. "Amos showed me: Jewelweed is a natural antidote for poison ivy. You can find it, spring through fall, in low moist areas like this. If you've rubbed against poison ivy, pick some jewelweed as you walk along. You can save jewelweed juice by crushing the leaves and freezing them in ice cube trays. Ruby uses a mortar and pestle; I use a blender."

"How will I recognize jewelweed again?" she asked.

"If you touch the orange flower, it pops. Its other name is Touch-me-not."

She drove Sam to his bus at the put-in at Conway's Ford. He was going up the valley further north to visit Farley Dodge. "For music lessons," he said.

When Grace turned to head south to the farm, she waved for Sam to stop. "You know," she said out her car window, "I feel this is the first time I've ever met anyone of my own species."

As she drove back to the farm, she braked as three wild turkeys strolled across the road. She was thinking—"Touch me, touch me not." Sam was physically compelling, but not intense. He was a scientist, but seemed gentle like an artist. She could not figure him out or her attraction to him.

She recovered from her reverie, "Touch me, touch-me-not," she laughed. Her car radio blared North Carolina soul music: "Stay Just a Little Bit Longer," and "She's Got That 39-21-40 Shape" by Maurice Williams and the Zodiacs. She was ready for somebody to touch her.

11

Rain beat on the tin roof of the farmhouse, thrumming cold and dark—insistent, demanding. In her bedroom under the eave of the roof, when it was raining, she had heard her parents arguing, yelling at each other again.

"Eleanor, get off your high horse," her father said.

"I'm leaving, Tommy," her mother had said.

"You've been drinking," he answered.

"I'm leaving for good."

"You can't go anywhere tonight, Ellie," he had said. "Water's rising after a week of rain." Rain was pelting the roof.

"I won't be stranded here in a flood," she said. "I'm dying of boredom."

"I won't let you shack up at the Homestead," he said.

"You can't stop me," Eleanor yelled. "I'm divorcing you."

"Quiet down, Ellie; don't be waking Grace."

But she was not awake; she was dreaming, seven years later, reliving this nightmare because of the rain on the tin roof. In her dream-memory the little girl Grace, tiptoeing down to sleep with Ruby, heard a thwack.

Did her father hit her mother? No, he would not do that; she might have slapped him, and he'd turn his cheek. Thwack again, a branch hit the roof in the wind.

"Listen to me, I'm leaving Grace with you," her mother had said. "You love her so much. I can't go back to college now with a child and a baby."

"A baby? Whose baby?" Her father's voice was ice.

Grace sat up in bed to stop the dream. The rain was pouring down, the wind knocking a branch onto the tin roof. She had been dreaming, but what she dreamed was real. She remembered her parents' last argument now. The dream could not be stopped because it was memory. That night over Ruby's snoring Grace had heard her mother's new sedan start and leave, but she lay still because her mother had said she did not want her. Then Grace heard her father come downstairs, and she got up again. Ruby, half-asleep, mumbled, "Leave them be, child."

On the kitchen table Grace had seen her mother's bottle, the one Ruby hid in the pantry. Her father was in the back hall, putting on his hunting coat.

"Don't go out tonight, Daddy," she had said, but he did not listen.

When he leaned down to kiss her goodbye, she caught the whiff of whiskey, which she knew from her mother, strange on her father's breath. "You stay here, Gracie. Go back to bed."

"Daddy, I can't sleep."

So Tom warmed some milk in a saucepan on the woodstove, stirred in chocolate powder, and poured it into a blue crock mug. He sat with Grace in the kitchen until she finished. He tousled her rusty curls, in his affectionate gesture, and pushed hair off her face, then left.

The dream brought back memories Grace had buried for seven years, and buried with the bad memory were her feelings. She had never been able to think about how her father had died.

Grace, age ten, had run out to yell at her Daddy starting his truck, his old green Chevy with rounded hood. "Daddy, don't go, the water is rising." She wailed, wet in her nightgown, shivering in the black rainstorm, "Daddy, come back."

Outside the sky, seven years earlier, had been pitch black, the swirling water tomb dark. Down the road, amid the wailing of wind and rain, the truck ignition had choked and whirred. Her father's old Chevy had stalled in the water rising over the low cement bridge at Brewers Notch. The windshield wipers fell separately out of synch—thwock, thwock—and the headlights glowed dim green in the black, wet night like aquarium lights.

Under the heavy rain on the tin roof, Grace now visualized her father turning the key again to start the truck so he could follow Eleanor to the Homestead. He may have intended to charge into that fancy resort in his hunting jacket and farm boots and

74

demand to know what room she was in. He would confront her, with whomever she had run off to meet.

Her father was never angry, but that night he would have been impatient with the old truck when it stalled on the ford and would have opened the door and stepped out into black water surging over the floorboard, above his knees, trying to suck him downriver. Letting go of the door handle, he lost his footing and slipped off the narrow bridge and was washed downriver in the current, flaying his arms against floating branches and debris to stay above water to breathe, fighting the cold water that sapped his strength.

My father was so young and strong and handsome, Grace thought. He could have swum the crest of a tidal wave. He must have hit his head when he had slipped and been swept downstream by the rush of the river, tumbling under water, cold and dark, until the tree branches caught his body.

Daddy, the water is rising.

Seven years later, Grace was shivering in bed as she was more awake. Rain beat on the roof and gushed down the drainpipes, relentless rain to wash canyons in the pastures and swell the river over its banks.

Daddy, the water is rising. Maybe he made no mistake, but died of a broken heart, when Eleanor left. But his life was so short.

Crying, Grace, age seventeen, ran downstairs, past Ruby's door, to the front porch to see how high the water was. The night was too dark. She tried to listen. If the water was rising, animals had to be herded to a higher field. Grace pulled on Ruby's rubber boots by the front door. She found no slicker. She ran through the front yard gate, getting soaked in her nightgown, climbed up and swung her legs over the pasture fence. She ran headlong down the eroded pasture and stumbled in a gully.

"Gawl-dangit," Grace cursed, as she had heard Ruby do, her breath knocked out for a minute and her knees bruised and muddy. She stood up and squinted her eyes to see in the dark and rain. She had forgotten her glasses by her bedside, not quite aware then if she were ten years old or seventeen. Now the fall had startled her awake; she was quite sure who and where she was, wet and cold and scared.

Her parents' yelling that night had been a bad dream Grace had forgotten. Seven years earlier, when she woke late in the morning in Ruby's bed, her hair still damp from rain, Amos and Ruby were quiet when she walked into the kitchen.

Right away Amos had said, "Grace, come here." He had hugged her. "Your father drowned last night. That means he's dead." She pulled away, but Amos held her until she absorbed what he had said.

Ruby had said, "Grace, why don't we go together to feed the chickens this morning?"

After a neighbor reported Tom's empty truck at daybreak blocking the road, the neighbor men had walked along the riverbank downstream of the bridge. In the morning after the flash flood, the stream looked so docile. When water receded, Amos found Tom's body tangled in branches leaning over the river. Amos carried Tom to the church hall, the closest building, and laid him on a dinner table. Amos had adored Tom like a brother— Tom who went off to war and college and brought back a society bride.

When Ruby had called Eleanor at the Homestead, she refused to come back. Ruby said, "Some man answered her room phone at the hotel."

"Bitch. Prissy, selfish bitch," Amos had said in the kitchen that morning. He had always blamed Eleanor for Tom's death. "That woman has a heart of ice," he said.

"Hush," Ruby said. "The child," nodding toward Grace in the sitting room where she was not supposed to hear the grownups, feeling guilty her father didn't love her enough to stay.

Her mother had never felt a smidgen of grief, and Grace wasn't supposed to show any. Eleanor had swept her away that afternoon with no dolls or clothes. Grace left Ruby without being able to say goodbye enough and left her dog Lady, the sheepdog with one blue eye and one brown eye.

The river sounded so loud. But the creekbank was dry. Grace heard Ruby calling from the house, so she ran back up to the porch.

"Oh, Ruby, I had a nightmare."

"Come inside. Law, child, you're soaked to the skin."

"It was raining like this the night my Daddy drowned."

"Come on," Ruby said. "You dry off and warm up." Ruby handed her a terry bathrobe. "Here, put this on. Now, what's this about?"

"It was my fault," Grace said in a shaky voice.

"Wait till you stop shivering before you talk," Ruby said. "Go ahead and cry," and Ruby rocked her for a long time till her crying sputtered out. "You had a bad dream."

"But it really happened. Eleanor ran off because she didn't want Daddy; she didn't want me either, she said. And Daddy followed her, but his truck stalled on the bridge and he washed downriver and drowned. It's my fault."

"Yes, that's what happened. But why do you think it is your fault?"

"I couldn't convince him to stay."

Ruby said, "You were barely ten."

"But, because I delayed him, he didn't get across the bridge before the flood water."

"Grace, honey, you can't blame yourself for other people's decisions,' Ruby said. "You can't blame yourself for what other people decide to do." Grace sniveled and wiped her nose on the sleeve. Ruby said, "Grace, have you ever mourned for your father?"

"My mother whisked me away from the farm that afternoon. I never thought about it before, I think I heard Eleanor say that night she was pregnant. But she never had any more babies."

Ruby said, "Don't cast blame either. Of course, I would like to take out your mother's . . . vanity bone."

Grace laughed, "You're right; the only tune she can sing is 'Me, me, me.'" They both laughed.

12

In the daylight, when Grace, age seventeen, woke in Ruby's bed, water drops from overhanging branches pinged on the porch roof. She sat up, realizing she had slept through the morning milking.

"My leg is feeling better," Ruby said, when Grace hurried into the kitchen. "Sam is parked down in the meadow if you want to see him."

Joining Sam on the step of his bus, she could see about ten feet in the fog.

"Don't burn your lip," he said, handing her the cup of his metal thermos. "The rim is hot."

A cloud enveloped the valley, as moist as driving through a car-wash tunnel. Grace could not see the river, but she could hear the water rolling over riffles.

"Just the water sound," she said, "isolated without the view, makes the river seem more alive, talking to us." The rocks by the riverbank were pastel like a Fair Isle sweater; gray-green lichen on gray granite turned pink when wet.

Grace said. "I'm still chilled from tripping around in the rain. I was pretty dumb."

"Ruby told me you'd been roaming outside last night. Let's find a hot spring to warm you up. Go get your bathing suit."

At the corner of two country highways, the Warm Springs Inn sat on a hill overlooking the village, six miles north and considerably less posh than the Homestead Hotel in Hot Springs, and the Warm Springs were not quite as hot. The inn served meals country style under the gaze of taxidermied deer and trophy trout. The bathhouses at Warm Springs were whitewashed round clapboard buildings, like Romanesque domed chapels.

By the road, Grace read the silver historic marker, "'The gentlemen's bath house, an octagon, was built in 1761, and the ladies', with its twenty sides, in 1836.'" She added, "Both look as if they haven't been painted since then."

"I thought Thomas Jefferson designed these places," Sam said, "but it doesn't say so. He must have bathed here, though; Stonewall Jackson and Robert E. Lee, too."

They parked in the small gravel lot next to the only other car. Green lawns surrounded the two old white wood structures, which covered pools of hot water diverted from a natural sulfur spring. Ancient attendants, a black man and woman, collected a dollar each from Sam and Grace. They looked shocked when he asked if they could use the same pool.

"Ladies and gentlemen may not share a bathhouse," the old lady said. Nobody else was around, but the rules forbade men and women together.

"These two must have been here since Jefferson's time," Grace whispered to Sam. "She is all wrinkled up like an apple-head doll. And his face is smooth like petrified wood, brown like mahogany."

The old woman sat in the sun outside the ladies' dressing room, guarding the door to keep her in and him out. Inside was dark; the unpainted wooden walls and benches looked full of splinters. Grace's bare feet, when she slipped off her sneakers and socks, were cold on the stone floor. She hung her jeans and sweater on a hook and pulled on her navy-blue nylon tank suit. On the wall above the bench, a faded metal sign, maybe from 1920, said, "Ladies must wear bathing costumes." She wondered if gentlemen could bathe in the buff.

The moist heat accosted her when she opened the door to the pool. The water was deserted and smelled strongly of sulfur. There was no lifeguard, but Grace did not want the old lady watching her. She held the handrail to keep from slipping down the stone stairs. The round pool, about thirty-five feet in diameter and four feet deep, was dug out of rock. She walked around keeping her hair dry, swirling her arms to her side and in front of her, as chill and fear seeped out of her. The hot water tired her like a drug; she had slept very little the night before. After circling the pool, she sat on the wood steps immersed to her neck, then leaned her hair back in the water. Looking up, she saw swallows darting in and out to feed baby birds in nests under the eaves, open to the sky.

Lulled in the hot pool, Grace wondered why did her Daddy ever love Eleanor? He should have let her leave that night. Sam had said the river can't damage you, but her father drowned. If you flow in its direction, Sam said. Daddy pushed the wrong way; he should have let her mother go. He was a calm man who never lost his temper, who one time got angry. A thought glanced across Grace's mind, Why keep blaming myself? But she buried it.

Grateful the storm of the night before had cleared, she went outside and lay on the grass in her bathing suit, soaking up May sun like a lizard. The hot sulfur spring flowed in two streams from a little pagoda across the lawn to the bathhouses. In the parking lot the old man soaped and rinsed his shiny green sedan, a model from the 1940s she did not recognize. The old lady dozed in her chair. The whole place had a sense of surviving a time warp. She wondered how to sneak past the gatekeepers to swim with Sam.

After a while, he came out of the men's bathhouse, his wet hair slicked down, and lay on the grass next to her. He had freckles all over his hairy chest and back. But she saw no Hobbit hair between his toes.

"Sam, do you reckon they're married?"

"Who?"

"The old couple who tend the baths?"

"Naw, but they sneak in the pool together at midnight and mess around."

"Sam, that's absurd," Grace said. "You know, this spring is more fun than the Country Club pool."

"Grace, how can you still belong to a country club?" he asked.

"My mother . . . "

"No, I mean you."

"I play tennis," she said.

"White club, white school, white church," he said.

"The Blacks want to go to separate churches with their own families and neighbors," she said.

"Do they? Grace, you're a sheltered little rich girl." Sam rolled over on his stomach.

She sputtered, "Why, I . . . ." Who did he think he was, from Georgia, telling her she was sheltered, when she had traveled alone to England?

"It's a wonder there's any metal left on that car," he said. The old black man waxed and polished the high sheen on his green car. "My father drives a car almost as old."

Sam got up and walked over to his bus and came back with a gallon of apple cider, which he offered to Grace, "Thirsty?" She tipped the plastic bottle and gulped the sweet cider.

"Thanks. What did you and your father fight about?" she asked.

"My mother had just died, and while she was dying, I forgot to apply to college; nobody was advising me. So, when I finished high school, my lottery number was low, like third in line; so when I turned eighteen, I was going to be drafted."

Sam sat with his elbows on his knees. "I refused to go to Vietnam, so I applied to be a conscientious objector and convinced my draft board I'm a pacifist. Before the Selective Service sent their greetings, I had already registered as a C.O."

She asked, "How did you get to be a pacifist?" Sam was more radical than any of the guys she knew in Richmond.

"I've seen enough senseless violence," Sam said. "My old man never stood up to anybody in his whole life, but called me a Communist when I refused to be drafted."

"What made you refuse to fight?" Grace asked.

"Maybe the moment I knew was when I was sixteen at a kids' camp where I taught canoeing and archery. One morning I yelled at some boys who were clowning around, pointing arrows at each other. I was angry," he breathed out to relax. "'Don't you realize this is a weapon?' I said, brandishing a bow; 'You could get hurt.' In the corner of my eye I saw a rabbit grazing by the bull's-eye, a hundred feet away, so I pulled my arrow taut in the bow, swung around, took a bead on it, and let fly."

He paused, "I wanted to prove a point. The boys had never seen me angry, so they stayed quiet. I walked down and picked up the arrow shaft with the rabbit body hanging slack from its neck, seeping warm blood. And I said, 'Now see, this could happen to you.' I didn't like what I had done one bit."

Sam leaned over and brushed some grass off her shoulder. "I thought soldiers turned into animals; actually animal predators have a lot more dignity. At camp that summer were two Vietnam veterans. After three tours of duty in Nam without a scratch, Murphy had been shot hitchhiking near Fort Bragg. He would roll around this bullet that was still under the skin of his wrist. The other vet, Doc, who ran the camp infirmary, had been a medic in the army. He boasted that he poured poison into Viet Cong prisoners' ears." Sam took another swig of cider.

"These two loony soldiers argued all summer, and Murphy tried to strangle Doc. It took all us teenage counselors to pull them apart. I have an impulsive temper myself, like my father, and I decided not to kill animals or people."

Grace had never seen Sam's temper. He seemed mild to her. Her mother's moods were unpredictable. Grace got scared when people got angry, as if it were her fault.

"Jared, my older stepbrother, got out of fighting in Vietnam because he was 4-F," she said. "He has gallstones, or flat feet. If the draft board had refused your appeal, would you have gone to jail or Canada?"

"I didn't have to. As a C.O., I did alternative service for two years, washing out bedpans in the mental hospital in Staunton."

"That sounds like a waste of time," she said.

"Naw, crazy people are happier than most of us. I could take a few courses for college credit. I worked with another C.O. orderly who was Quaker, and I learned a lot about patience from him and the patients. I mean, this guy acted according to his convictions that all people are equal. I attended Quaker Meeting with him and, when I started at UVa, I joined the Charlottesville Friends Meeting."

Grace said, "You're the first Quaker I've met."

"It's not like I became a Quaker suddenly, but rather that I met other people who think the way I do. I went to a potluck at someone's farm, and there were nine kinds of pie spread on tables under the trees. That's values: nine pies. And Chester, the clerk of Charlottesville Meeting, a small man with a white goatee, calls country dances in five languages."

"I mean, what do Quakers believe?" she asked.

"Quakers have no dogma," Sam said. "Most Friends agree on three main ideas. First, there's an Inner Light in each of us. Second, all people are equal. Third, God can talk to each of us every day, updating Scripture and eliminating need for a hired preacher. We meet in silence."

"I would like to learn to sit still," Grace said.

"George Fox started the Quakers in England in the 1640s," he said. "The name 'Quaker' was an insult originally—quaking with spirit, and the name stuck. Because Quakers wouldn't take their hats off to judges—because no person is better than another— Quakers got thrown in jail a lot."

"How about playing cards and dancing?"

"To guide us are testimonies—like equality, simplicity, integrity. Because we should be honest all the time, we don't swear on the Bible to tell the truth. If I go to court, I can say 'I affirm.' We work for prison reform and for education. A lot of Quakers are scientists."

"Like you," Grace said.

"As pacifists, Quakers have been conscientious objectors for three hundred years," he said. "George Fox said, 'We must learn to take away the occasion for war.'"

She said. "Okay, but how?"

"Respond with love to anger, so that violence is less possible."

"How about your father?" Grace asked. "How do you deal

with his anger?"

"Try to see the fear and sadness beneath his temper, but I don't succeed very well," he said. "I've given up trying to talk to him. For me, my family are people who love me, like Ruby."

A shadow had crept up the wall to cover the old lady leaning against the bathhouse. She roused herself from her nap and moved her wooden chair five feet to the left and sat in the sun again.

Sam said. "I'm working on being peaceful inside, but politics angers me. In ecology I study how the community of aquatic insects thrives in competition. If I get mad at government, I'll fight politicians with good data." He stood up, "Hey, are you dry yet? Let's head out."

In the dressing room, Grace took off her bathing suit and pulled on her jeans, shirt, and sweater. She found no mirror to straighten her hair. She carried her sneakers and socks to the bus. The grass felt good on her bare feet.

The ignition of the VW bus was slow turning over. "I think I can. I think I can," urged Sam, and the engine rumbled alive. "Stubborn engine when the weather's damp."

In the bus, driving back to the farm, he said, "Conscientious objectors are not just young men who refuse the draft, but anyone who won't work for weapon manufacturers or invest in military companies. Being a pacifist doesn't mean to stop fighting. In fact, a conscience makes me aware of battles that need fighting peaceably." He said, "Any person can act according to conscience, like opposing the dam in your valley."

"But, if our battle is against the dam, we should stop using electricity. I'm not that noble," Grace said. "The irony is that Ruby and I can get by just fine without power on Jack Creek, but we're going to lose our homes for air conditioners in Dayton, Ohio."

"Aren't you angry?"

"I sure am," she said. "I mean, look at these trees and pastures."

"So protect 'em," he said. "Stop the dam."

"But I was taught to respect the government," Grace said.

"Our democracy requires participation," Sam said. "I'm not saying to pour sugar in their gas tanks; but be a citizen. You're the ditziest woman sometimes, Grace."

"Well, that's my mother's southern-belle training: let men think they're smarter than I am."

"There's no way I'm as bright as you are, Grace," Sam said. "You pick up everything I say. You're always questioning everyone. The only way I won't respect you is if you purposely hide or waste your intelligence."

He shifted down for Ruby's steep driveway and stopped his bus in the yard.

"But I was raised not to raise a fuss in public," Grace said.

"Use your best tools. You're a southern belle, right? Show your stuff. Win the highlanders' trust; use your charm and brains, and exploit your Richmond connections. But do your homework. Find the opponent's soft belly, his Achilles heel. Be radical, from the Latin meaning. What did your father teach you? Grace, use your roots."

While Sam went inside to say goodbye to Ruby, Grace watched cardinals and wrens at the feeder. When he came back out, she asked him, "When will I know what to do? How will I know?"

He said, "When William Penn decided to become a Quaker, he asked George Fox if he could still wear a sword, because gentlemen in the seventeenth century attached long sabers to their belts, so long they could trip over them. And George Fox told Penn, 'Wear your sword as long as you can.'"

Sam hugged her goodbye, "That means, Grace, follow your vanity until your conscience speaks louder."

13

What Grace liked best about downtown Richmond were fading painted signs on brick warehouses. She could smell Smithfield hams, Sauer's spices, Liggett & Meyers tobacco, and FFV cookies. FFV originally stood for "First Families of Virginia," but the cookie-factory wall advertised "Finest Flavor in Virginia." The best smell in Richmond was the Wonder Bread factory on Cary Street across from the Thomas Jefferson Hotel, where she'd heard they had filmed Scarlet O'Hara falling down the red staircase in *Gone With The Wind*. "Wonder Bread Builds Bodies 12 Ways" was the slogan. Grace wondered which twelve ways. White bread, she knew from Ruby, had little nutrition, but Wonder Bread was good for wadding into balls to throw to ducks at Maymont Park.

Tolly's law office was on the second floor of a bank building overlooking the corner of Ninth and Main, the center of Richmond's financial district. Grace parked her car in his garage off Ninth Street. Living in McDowell County, she hadn't seen men wearing three-piece suits in a long time. She remembered the previous summer walking down Main Street with Jared. He had turned into Tolly's tailor and ordered a white linen suit.

"Good for mint juleps," he said, and, "Charge it to Spotswood." Spotswood was Jared's mother, Tolly's first wife.

"You can't do that," Grace exclaimed. "You're twenty-three years old. Pay for it yourself."

"I can until Spotswood stops me. I'll let her pay for my gas and liquor and clothes, as long as she's willing, and tuition for business school."

Grace was glad she did not have to depend on Eleanor to support her, but had her own trust fund from Charlotte Dabney, her mother's mother. Well, what was the difference, if she and Jared both lived off family money? Grace felt slightly smug she didn't throw money around like Eleanor and Jared. Eleanor had more in common with her stepson than with her own daughter.

In the bank lobby, Grace pushed the elevator button to the

top floor. The vice president of Commonwealth Utility and Power Company had agreed to see Grace because he played golf with her stepfather. When the elevator door opened, she approached the receptionist's antique table set in the middle of a pastel Persian rug. With a little headphone attached to her ears, so she could use both hands writing messages, she gestured Grace to follow. She wore stockings and dress shoes for the first time in months, camouflaged as a Richmond young lady so that Winston Wood would listen better to what she had to say.

Mr. Wood's secretary, a well-groomed woman of fifty, led Grace down a corridor with horse-and-hound hunting prints on the wall. She sat on the edge of the wing chair, feet crossed at her ankles, as if she were called out of class to see the principal. While waiting, she looked out the glass wall of windows on the twelfth floor over the bend of the James River. In England, when she had looked east from London toward Richmond, she had recognized that same bend in the Thames River, and recognized that the similar view must be why British settlers had named Virginia's capital, Richmond.

Shortly, Winston Wood came to his door to beckon her. He was an elegant, white-haired gentleman in a gray suit. "Mr. Wood, thank you for seeing me." She shook his hand.

"I'm glad to meet you. How is your lovely mother?" He ushered her to a brown leather sofa by a cherry-wood coffee table with two neat piles of glossy magazines and annual reports. An eight-foot schefflera tree stood in a pot by the panoramic windows.

"Why, just fine," she answered. She was sure Mr. Wood ate dinner with her parents at the Country Club every week.

"Now what is it you have come to find out?" He did not say anything about her not selling land early as her stepfather had arranged.

"I'm really interested in learning about the dam CUPCO wants to build on Jack Creek," she said. "I own land there. Can you tell me why you need the dam?"

"Oh, yes, the McDowell County Project. We need to expand

our electric-generating capacity to meet peak-load demand. Everyone turns on appliances at the same time. We need more power when people get home in the afternoon and turn on televisions and washing machines. We all want our air conditioners in the summer."

"What about saving electricity that isn't used in the middle of the night?" she asked.

"Fine idea, but that won't work yet," Wood answered, "until somebody creates a big-enough storage battery. And we don't want to build any more coal-fired plants because of air pollution, nor another oil-burning plant because the Arabs keep charging more for their oil. Besides the process is too costly, too inefficient to turn our oil or coal-fired plants on and off. They require a day or two to get on line."

"So why a dam?"

"It's not just one dam, but two dams," Wood explained. "A pump-storage hydroelectric system can store power," Wood explained. "Come and look at the model."

He stood and walked to a four-foot-square relief map of Jack Creek Valley. Grace recognized Bluff Mountain and the narrow valley and the high steep ridge of Potter Mountain to the east. But in place of her farm was the massive concrete structure of the second dam like an Egyptian pyramid.

Wood said, "There will be an upper reservoir on top of Bluff Mountain and a lower reservoir in the valley. Between them will be six 30-foot-diameter tunnels 500 feet long. We'll get power for peak-demand periods when water tumbles down through the turbines in the middle of the mountain." Wood was proud of the design. "During periods of low electrical usage, the turbines will reverse and pump water back up to the upper reservoir."

"But there's no water on top of the mountain," she said.

"Right. What's good about this site is the long drop from the top of the mountain to the valley," Wood explained. "There's no natural water source on top of Bluff Mountain now, you're right, but we'll pump water up there from the river."

"There's not a whole lot of water in Jack Creek either," Grace said.

"We know that. Our hydrologists tell us it will take a year to fill the lower reservoir, at forty-eight inches of rainfall a year, then a second year to pump water to the upper reservoir."

"What if it doesn't rain that year?" she asked.

"Then filling the reservoirs will take longer," Wood said. "The project will control flooding downstream. The whole time, the lower dam must release the minimum natural flow of water down river to keep fish alive." He sounded reasonable.

"Won't you waste electricity sending the water uphill?"

"Not waste necessarily. We'll use surplus power that wouldn't be used during a low-demand period. Surplus power in the middle of the night otherwise does go to waste."

"How big is this whole project?" Grace asked, as she swept her hand over the model of her valley.

"The area is five thousand acres, three thousand of which are on National Forest land. The rest is low-intensity agriculture and timberland on privately-owned land. But we'll compensate all the landowners generously."

Grace did not trust herself to comment as politely as she had resolved to do. She wanted to learn everything she could without blowing her cool.

"Mr. Wood, how will the project benefit folks who live in McDowell County?" she asked.

"Unemployment in McDowell County is highest in the state. During five years of construction, this project will provide jobs to two hundred men. The capital investment will increase the tax base of the county. Because the drawdown of water in the lower reservoir will be ten feet and in the upper reservoir, as much as thirty feet, we'll fence off the reservoirs to protect the public. Downstream we will build a smaller lake for water sports, and we'll build a picnic area and campground."

What about the yellow flowers and ferns growing on the cliff in the river canyon, and the otter slides? Grace wanted to ask. And her Daddy's grave?

But she thanked Mr. Wood and went off to fight afternoon traffic driving west on Main Street. After two months in the country, stoplights and noise were a hassle. She stopped at an outdoor-outfitter store. Lured by neon colors of nylon fabric, Grace bought a leaf-green tent, blue backpack, and purple down sleeping bag.

Grace was in no hurry to get to her mother's house. Before dinner would be endless polite cocktails. She was embarrassed to see Jared after their conversation the last night before she had flown to England. However, if he took her out, she might avoid getting into an argument with Tolly.

14

In high school Grace had started bucking her stepfather's authority. Since she moved to Richmond, she had walked along the James River below their house. Suddenly when she was fifteen, Tolly forbade her to walk alone, because she might "get attacked."

"You can't deny me the woods and the river," Grace stated unflustered. "I go to be alone. Besides, Dylan will protect me." Her English setter went everywhere with her, except to school. She continued walking along the railroad tracks by the canal, and Tolly did not stop her.

But since Dylan her dog had died last year, Eleanor's house always seemed emptier. Grace dropped her overnight bag on a bench in the front hall and went through the dining room for a cup of tea with Ophelia, just like old times. Eleanor had rarely been home in the afternoon when Grace returned from school, and while cooking dinner, Ophelia had supervised her homework and listened to middle-school heartbreaks.

In the kitchen Grace kicked off her heels and sat still five minutes. At work, Ophelia wore gray uniforms with white aprons. Even though Eleanor treated Ophelia like an employee, Grace thought of her as a member of her family. As a little girl, Grace had been startled the first time she saw Ophelia looking fashionable in a colored print dress at the bus stop—so Grace realized Ophelia had her own house and her own family, and cooking for Eleanor was not her whole life.

"How's your new grandbaby, Ophelia?" Grace asked her now.

"Fat and happy baby. Living in the country makes you look strong and happy, Grace," Ophelia told her. "Your mama expects you home for cocktails."

"Traffic makes me claustrophobic," Grace said. "I've got to get outside for an hour. Let me change out of city clothes.

"Hanging in your closet is a dress for you to wear tonight,"

93

Ophelia said, and Grace started up the back stairs from the pantry barefoot, then returned to pick up her shoes.

"Thanks, Ophelia."

Upstairs in her bedroom Grace dropped her skirt on the floor and pulled on some jeans and tennis shoes. Her closet was full of Richmond clothes. She had a dozen long party dresses for debutante parties, and as many tennis dresses. On the closet floor were shoes dyed to match pastel linen church dresses.

"Be back by six-thirty," Ophelia admonished, as Grace ran through the kitchen, grabbed a fistful of oatmeal cookies, yelled "Thanks, Ophelia," and headed out the back door. She walked down the hill of irises behind their house and cut across the neighbor's terraced azalea garden. She used to carry books to read outdoors, away from Eleanor's comment, "Don't keep your nose in a book all the time."

Grace missed Dylan, her after-school companion, sniffing animal trails. On another neighbor's property she noticed some strange yellow flags on metal stakes stuck in the ground. She walked down a lane of overhanging dogwood blossoms, which led to a bridge across the canal to the floodplain pastures.

When George Washington was a teenager, he had surveyed the Kanawha Canal to bypass rapids in the James River at the head of navigation in Richmond. Railroad tracks now followed the towpath west where mules used to drag barges upstream to the mountains.

Every few days a coal train passed along the canal. Running east, it was full of coal for the port at Hampton Roads, and heading west, the coal cars rattled by empty. Grace never figured out if the coal train had a set schedule. Sometimes after school she would sit on the hill above the canal, count over a hundred cars in the train, and wave to the caboose. But the train had never passed when she walked the tracks, and Grace had never seen anyone else there. Hoboes didn't jump the coal train to West Virginia. No suspicious characters wanted to attack her, as Tolly imagined.

To keep from tripping on the railroad tracks, she bobbed

along with an uneven gait. When she was smaller, her feet hit every crosstie. Now she was too tall to hit every tie and too short to hit every other. The necessary concentration cleared her mind of worrying about the dam that would flood her farm.

Eventually she tired of uneven railroad ties and walked along the towpath. In the weeds were fiddlehead ferns too old to eat. By the track was a smoldering chunk of charcoal that had jumped off the train. Grace stomped out the two-foot diameter circle of charred grass and tossed the football of coal, glowing on one end, into the canal. She commended herself for stopping a wildfire, Smokey the Bear, though no fire would have crossed the canal to the houses up the hill without a sharp wind.

A year ago, by the tracks, her dog Dylan had pointed to the skeleton of a dog, the size of a Labrador. The bones were clean, white and dry; the dog had been dead for a long time. Grace memorized the phone number on the dog collar. That night she had called to tell the family not to wait any longer for their dog to come home.

At the pasture gate she debated whether to walk farther and be late for her mother's cocktail hour. Several wealthy families owned the floodplain between the canal and the river. Grace was grateful for privileged access to open space in the city, five minutes from her house. If a caretaker ever questioned her, she only had to say she was Charlotte Dabney's granddaughter.

She would risk being late. She was careful to close gates although there were no cows grazing the pastures. The landowners grew corn to attract doves. During fall hunting season Grace was wary of walking across the fields. Only because rich people kept this floodplain for sport did it stay undeveloped. On the riverbank thick vines of poison ivy strangled the trees. Floods washed the banks of the river each spring, and debris up the bank and mud on the tree trunks showed the height of past floodwaters. In this spring's drought there had been no flood, and no need for flood protection by building a dam on Jack Creek.

Flood protection downstream was one reason the power

company gave to justify the dam on Jack Creek at the headwaters of the James. But floodplains are designed for holding floodwaters. Floods leave rich alluvial soil that is good for agriculture. But runoff from paved shopping malls or subdivisions channeled more water downriver, so downstream cities cried for dams upstream.

Grace fussed, Why aren't planners more aware of natural relationships? Ecology, Sam was teaching her, leads to awareness of choice and consequences.

A mile west, she came to Williams Dam and sat on the stone wall twenty feet above the spillway. Her old bamboo fishing rod was no longer hidden behind a bush. She had never caught a fish there, but didn't mind. She dangled her feet, beating her calves against the cool stone. Grace hummed a fiddle tune. The roar of noise cooled her as much as the wind from falling water.

Was Sam too old for her as a potential boyfriend, or not serious enough? It wasn't just his lack of money. He was not rushing to finish college and get a job. Did success matter to Grace? Yes, it did. She wanted a sweetheart with poise enough to belong anywhere. But Sam always felt comfortable, unconcerned how he looked to others. Would she be uncomfortable bringing him to the Country Club in Richmond? Or, maybe she was being critical because she was afraid of loving anyone else who would leave her.

The path along the riverbank led west toward the mountains. When Tolly told her she must not endanger herself walking alone by the railroad tracks, Grace never gave a thought to staying away from the river. She did not like anyone to tell her what she couldn't do.

When she entered the glass porch that evening, wearing the dress that Ophelia had ironed, Eleanor scolded immediately, "Grace Dabney, you do look like a tramp. Your hair needs styling. I'll make an appointment for you in the morning. You must pay more attention to your appearance."

Grace noticed Eleanor's cigarette ash was about to drop on the salmon paisley sofa cushion and leaned over with a pewter ashtray for her mother to flick off an ash.

"No, Eleanor, I'm spending tomorrow in the library to finish a paper, so I can graduate."

Tolly poured a daiquiri from a pitcher and handed the glass to Grace. She put it on an end table and didn't touch it again.

"You'll never meet a husband in the library, dear," Eleanor said. "No one wants to marry an egghead. Can't you take off those eyeglasses?"

"No, Eleanor, I am nearsighted. I need them to see."

"Why don't you get contact lenses, then?"

"I lost a lens in England and haven't replaced it yet." Grace changed the subject, "What are those little yellow flags on the hill behind the Cruikshank place?"

"Old Mrs. Cruikshank finally died," Tolly answered. "And she left her estate to her yardman. How old was she, dear? Ninety-five?"

Eleanor said, "The old house will be torn down, and her wretched yardman will move to Florida with the money he inherited." On her walks Grace used to talk to Tony, the gardener.

"What about the land?" she asked impatiently, before Eleanor could digress about Mrs. Cruikshank's social *faux pas*.

"Her estate is selling off eighteen acres in three-acre lots," Tolly said. "Don't worry. Million-dollar houses will be assets to the neighborhood."

"But those are my woods, that I walk." The raccoons and rabbits whose trails Dylan followed would have to move someplace else.

Ophelia came to the door of the porch to call Tolly to the telephone, and he walked into the living room.

"Not only was the yardman Portuguese; he was Catholic," Eleanor kept talking about Mrs. Cruikshank's gardener.

"You're such a snob," Grace muttered. With Tolly gone, both dropped their veneer.

"Why do you waste your time in that wretched outpost when I need you down here?" Eleanor said. Grace could never understand why Eleanor wanted her company.

"I want to restore the orchard," Grace said. "No one has tended the apple trees since Daddy died. The extension agent is advising me."

"Oh, spare me," Eleanor protested, waving away what she did not want to hear.

"Listen, Eleanor," she said squarely. "I'm trying to stop the Jack Creek dam so I can keep the farm long enough for me to understand where I come from. So I can remember when I was a little girl."

Eleanor behaved as if she would just as soon forget her daughter's whole name, Grace Dabney McAuley, and ignored that she had ever married Tom McAuley. When Eleanor remarried, Grace had refused, even at ten, to change her last name to Taliaferro.

Eleanor asked her, "Don't you have any nicer clothes? You must dress better than other girls. Let them know how rich you are."

Eleanor's definition of a lady was someone who makes people feel she is better than they are. Grace was developing a different sense of gentility. Living in the hills, she was beginning to see that a true lady is someone like Ruby who makes everyone else feel comfortable around her, who offers or accepts hospitality no matter how poor the house.

Eleanor kept lecturing. "Grace, you must remember it's just as easy to fall in love with someone rich."

"You didn't," Grace said. "You know, Eleanor, Tolly only married you for your money."

"Nonsense, don't say things to hurt my feelings," Eleanor said. "And even if he doesn't have any money of his own, he comes from a good background. For goodness sake, do marry someone with good breeding."

"You mean 'FFV'?" she quipped. Eleanor came from a fine Richmond family.

"Don't sass me," Eleanor said.

Just then, Jared swept in, wearing a pink Lacoste shirt and madras pants. "Oh Eleanor, don't you look lovely tonight." He leaned over to kiss Eleanor's cheek. Grace would not have been surprised if Jared kissed his stepmother's hand. These two men paid court to Eleanor as if she were the queen.

"Nice to see you, Grace," Jared said. "Are you really going to graduate?" He kissed her cheek too, then poured himself a drink at the butler's-tray table.

"Don't remind me I'm old enough to have a grown-up daughter," Eleanor whined.

"Oh Eleanor, you two look like sisters," Jared said, sitting on the salmon sofa next to her.

Officially, Jared lived with Spotswood in her country house in Aylett, twenty-five miles east of Richmond, but maintained a room in Eleanor and Tolly's Richmond house. He was away at prep school when Tolly married Eleanor. She flirted with him like every other man.

"Oh, Jared, it's a pity we aren't dining together tonight, but I must attend some business affair of Tolly's. Do be a dear and look after Grace Dabney. Take her to meet some nice people so she will forget that silly farm."

Grace felt smug. Like Shakespeare's Cordelia, she could not pay false compliments as Tolly and Jared did. If asked, like King Lear's honest daughter, Grace would have said, "Why I love you only as much as a daughter should."

15

"How come you don't have a date tonight?" Jared pestered Grace as he drove his racing-green MG to Dickie's house after cocktail hour.

"Why don't *you* have a date tonight?" she echoed. "Are you still seeing Connie?" She had liked the girl Jared took out the summer before.

"Oh no," he answered, "I don't want her to get spoiled."

"Why can't you be friends?" she asked. "You know, find a girl you can talk to." As much as she liked her stepbrother, he never treated his girlfriends as equals.

"My goodness, have you stopped shaving your legs?" he blurted out. "What is your new style, *nouveau pauvre*? Do you dress from an attic?" His criticism of her appearance always stung deep.

Despite Jared's best efforts, Grace failed at being "cool." She was still a bookworm and a tomboy. After her mother and his father got married, when no one else was paying any attention to Grace, Jared tried to coach her. When she was twelve, he had bought her first pair of Levis, helped her bleach them to look worn, and scald them to shrink. When she was fourteen, he had tried to teach her to smoke, but she kept coughing.

Jared had given Grace her first beer and explained that Richmond poise meant being able to drink like a fish. But a southern girl should stay sober enough to defend her virtue and to drive herself home. He had taught her to drive a gearshift car, balancing the clutch on the hill by the Edgar Cayce place at Virginia Beach, so she could always drive when her date was drunk.

"Southern fathers and brothers are protective of their women," Jared had said. Even before she was old enough, Grace had driven him home plenty of times, when he was too drunk.

At the front door of the stately Georgian brick house out River Road, Dickie greeted her, "Aha, Jared's little sister has grown tits," killing her resolution to get along in Richmond.

Jared, behind her, just chuckled, "She's been milking cows at her farm."

Each year, at the end of May, Dickie hosted a "roll-up-your-sleeves" barbecue, with greasy pork ribs, corn on the cob, coleslaw, and no utensils. Amazingly, when grease dripped from everyone's fingers and chins, Jared stayed clean. Sooner or later, somebody pushed Dickie in the swimming pool, and twenty more jokers jumped in to wash off barbecue sauce. The next morning Dickie's father's yardman would drain the pool to scrub off the ring of grease.

Three Morgan approached Grace to push her in. "Don't you dare," she warned and backed off to watch. So named because he had stuffy last names as first names, "so-and-so the third," Three was the only one of Jared's friends who treated her like a human. As a little sister, she was off limits. His crowd had enough gallantry that they wouldn't mess with anybody's sister. Grace was the only girl who arrived at their parties without a date. She could never keep track of the different girls with Jared's friends, except for skinny Dinah, who had dated Dickie since high school.

After midnight, four hard-core drinkers, and Grace, lounged in red-leather sofas in Dickie's father's library. Leather-bound law books lined the walls of the room where Jared's crowd drank all night long, all through high school and college, because Mr. Grimes, Dickie's widowed father, never kicked them out.

"Jared, can you please drive me home?" she asked.

"Relax, be a good sport," he answered jovially.

Dickie moved the brass fire screen to light the ornamental birch logs. His wet blue seersucker shorts and yellow Oxford shirt dripped on the Oriental rug. He pulled his wallet out of his shorts and wrung out a ten-dollar bill. "Can't start a fire with this," he said.

"Save your money for betting on the horses," Jared said. "Montpelier Races are Saturday, and Sunday is tennis at the Lindbergs'."

While he was in Dickie's kitchen mixing rum and fruit in the blender, Grace rolled the huge globe by the sofa. She wondered where Will Parker was. On the globe she traced the path she had flown from Richmond to Philadelphia and across the ocean to London. She knelt on the thick rug to trace routes of trips she had taken from London to Paris and Munich. With all that distance there and back again, what had she learned?

In London, no one knew her Richmond family, and she didn't have to impress anyone. Simple household responsibilities helped Grace trust her own judgment. She paid her own bill down at the corner chemist, what the English call a drug store, and could stew chicken on the one-ring burner in the school's common room.

Seeing Jared with all his friends, Grace could measure that she had grown a lot in a year, and outgrown his crowd. These older boys had impressed her before; but now she had met a serious guy like Will, who was studying at Princeton and London School of Economics. Will said he liked her smart, and so did Sam, but did they mean it? Even smart guys end up with dumb wives.

Turning the old leather globe, she noticed how many names of countries and national boundaries had changed, especially in Africa—Congo to Zaire, Rhodesia to Zimbabwe. The world didn't matter here though, she thought. To Jared, Virginia was the center of the universe, still in the eighteenth century. In West End Richmond, THE High School was Episcopal High School in Alexandria, THE University was Charlottesville; THE River meant Fishing Bay Yacht Club in Deltaville, THE Beach was the Princess Anne Club at Virginia Beach.

So refined and so uncouth, Jared delivered a bright-red rum concoction, which he christened a "Bombay Bunghole." Dickie was playing a record by Doug Clark and the Hot Nuts: "Nuts, hot nuts, get 'em from the peanut man."

Jared was telling a business school story: "Benjamin Franklin said to avoid the appearance of dishonesty. I do not recall that he ever said, don't be dishonest."

She said, "Jared, the world has changed."

"Not my world," he said. "No blacks work in Tolly's office

on Main Street."

"Jared! That's outrageous," she said. "I can see Tolly's being prejudiced because he grew up in a different era. But you, Jared, you live in Richmond a hundred years ago." His favorite post-midnight drive was touring the seven hills of Richmond: Gambles, Navy, Shockoe, Frenchman's Garden, Church Hill, and Council Chamber. Grace counted to remember all the names. She could perceive her stepbrother, as she had not done before. He was a bigot as well as a peacock.

Since last summer, she distanced herself from him. Jared had carried his responsibility for her social education too far the night before she flew to England. After she finished packing, they sat in the den in Eleanor's house. Grace was tired, but she valued times when he dropped his guard of coolness.

"When you travel," he had advised her, "learn to cook the local cuisine. Sample the fine wines and take a lover in every country. You better get some birth control pills before you leave."

"Oh, Jared, you're drunk," she said.

"I'll bet Eleanor has never explained sex to you," Jared said. He was right. Eleanor was too uptight to think about anyone's problems but her own.

Before Grace went up for a blind date with a freshman in Jared's fraternity, she had overheard Tolly telling Eleanor, "Have you had a talk with your daughter about the facts of life?"

Eleanor had answered, "Oh, don't worry, I'll talk to her sometime," and she never did. Grace had read the mechanics in a book.

The night before she flew to London, Jared had said, "I'll explain to you about making love."

"No thank you. No," she said. She couldn't believe he was saying this. He was really sloshed.

"This is the time of your life to experiment," he had said. "Have fun without Richmond watching."

"Good night," Grace said, standing up. "I'm flying at the crack of dawn." Jared reached for her, clenched her wrist, and held her there.

"Let me tell you," he said, "so you can be prepared."

Grace couldn't believe he aimed to give her a blow-by-blow account. She pulled away and ran upstairs. The next morning when she left for the airport, he was still asleep.

In Dickie's library, Jared asked her, "So, did you fall in love in England?" For the first time, she had a sense he would be jealous if she told him yes.

She shook her head. In London she had been snowed over Will, but now he seemed distant. Maybe she only wanted to show him off to Jared. Will was an economist and awfully practical. Sam was a scientist and philosophic.

"How about now?" Jared asked her. "Have you found a hillbilly boyfriend?"

"I go to bed at dark and get up at dawn to milk the cow." She was willing for Jared to make fun of Jers, but not Sam. "I'm not used to staying up this late. I'm driving myself home, and you can catch a ride."

Thursday morning, Grace re-read Wordsworth's poems, "Tintern Abbey" and "Ode on Immortality." Could she submit a paper that said she *liked* them? Had she lost her academic edge by working two months on the farm?

The previous fall in England, on the way from Bath to Wales, Grace had visited the ruins of Tintern Abbey. She was pleased that the stone church had walls, but no roof and a grass floor. Gothic arched windows opened to blue sky. Like Wordsworth, Grace had climbed the hill that overlooked the ruined abbey being reclaimed by nature. The view of Tintern Abbey resembled the view from the top of her farm's orchard, and the poem talked about a mountain spring, lofty cliffs, a pastoral farm, plots of cottage ground like Jack Creek Valley.

When Grace had first read Wordsworth's poem, intuitions flew to her, whizzing above words, "My heart leaps up when I behold a rainbow in the sky." The poem described three stages of life: the youth ran around the woods, splashed by the waterfall. The older person walked in nature, thinking about truth and beauty. The old man remembered his youth in nature and glimpsed transcendent truths. Grace would think better outside, but she had no more time.

In the University of Richmond library she reviewed her notes. She pulled all her bushy hair back from her face and secured it in a knot at the top of her head. A psychology article about childhood and imagination said a child's early conscience grows from closeness to nature. Grace herself had lived her first decade on the farm. If a child felt connected to the outside world and also separate, the article said, she could grow as an individual. She had developed her own emotions just so far but stopped when her father died.

"Wordsworth," she had written in notes, "depicted an idyllic childhood as his impulse to be creative." As an adult, Wordsworth had tapped nature as his source of creative power. His genius came from the ability to remember childhood. As his memory led to poetic imagery, landscape became language. Satisfied she could write a decent paper, Grace tucked her pencils in her bun of hair.

In a carrel in the library stacks she typed an eight-page paper direct from her notes, throwing in lots of Wordsworth's quotes to pad it and citing the psychology article. This psychological approach to Wordsworth gave clues to her own feelings. Grace had built her own intuition and ethics playing games with her father on the farm and in the woods, but at his death her emotions had closed up shop. The memory she lacked was a riddle she couldn't solve.

"Good enough," she spoke out loud in the library carrel as she typed a title page last. Her watch said three o'clock. She drove the paper to her English teacher's office at St. Catherine's, with a whole two hours to spare.

Friday morning, Eleanor's hairdresser cut Grace's hair and shellacked her curls in place for the Friday night graduation. Grace wanted to wash her hair, but Eleanor would have killed her. Like the forty other girls in her class, she wore a long white dress and carried a dozen red roses. She won a book of poetry as a research award. When she got home, she washed the varnish out of her hair.

Grace had applied and been accepted early decision to Sweet Briar College before she left for fall semester in England. If she wanted to be a scholar and a teacher, Grace did not think she belonged at Sweet Briar, where being blonde mattered more than grades.

16

In Richmond, Grace woke two hours after milking time at the farm. Ruby would cover the cows until she got back. After breakfast alone in the kitchen, she loaded her stuff and drove west to the steeplechase at Montpelier. Jared had already left to ride up with Dickie and Dinah. Not even Ophelia was around to say goodbye.

On Interstate 64, Grace felt glad to be heading uphill. Driving west held tender significance for her—either escape or arrival. There was always something magic about her first glimpse of the Southwest Mountains, east of Charlottesville, where Jefferson had built Monticello. Even if she were alone, Grace felt she won a prize for seeing the mountains first, as if her father were in the car playing games.

At Zions Crossroads, she turned north on Route 15. The red-clay mud along the road-cut told her she had left Tidewater and was in the Piedmont. In Gordonsville she turned west on Route 20. Along the road to Montpelier all the houses for half a mile, including the old train station, were painted forest green with white shutters. Either Mrs. Scott owned all the houses in the feudal village or gave everybody the same green paint. Mrs. Scott played the part of nobility; she had doubled the original Montpelier estate house to fifty-five rooms.

Marion duPont Scott had married Randolph Scott, Virginia gentleman turned Hollywood cowboy star in the first talking Western movies. Mrs. Scott was more than eighty years old and had divorced Randolph decades earlier. Grace drove through the gates of the estate and parked in the General Admission area. In the cordoned-off VIP area, she passed tailgate picnics in woody station wagons and large dark sedans. She spotted Dickie's red Mustang convertible with the trunk open to a full bar. Champagne was spilling from a bottle Jared had just uncorked.

"You're right on time. The sun is over the yardarm," he

toasted Grace as she walked up. "Here comes Marion to review the crowds." Out of sight in the back of a little black carriage, drawn by four chestnut horses, Mrs. Scott rode by the paddock. "Rumor has it Randolph was unfaithful in Hollywood, so she bought Dolley Madison's house."

Next to Dickie's Mustang was Karen and Buzzy Baskerville's Country Squire. "Help yourself," Karen greeted Grace, indicating trays of deli salads spread on a card table between the cars. "We have fried chicken enough for the Russian army." Married six years, Karen and Buzzy had left their five children, including two sets of twins, at home with a nanny.

Grace cut a slice of coconut layer cake from Patterson Avenue Bakery. Jared brought liquor and his battery-operated blender to mix rum-and-fruit drinks with bizarre names. Nobody was paying attention to the horses. When the starting gun fired, Grace, Dinah, Dickie, and Jared ambled to the fence to watch them run close by.

"This race is the second of five," he said. "The Morgans' horse is running later."

"What horses have you bet on?" Dickie asked Jared. "Where's the betting table?"

"Over at the tent."

The Montpelier steeplechase was manicured like a golf course and landscaped with water ditches and boxwood hedges. Twelve horses raced out of view behind a stand of trees, then back over the crest of hill a quarter mile away. The Appalachian Mountains hovered faint above the western horizon as a blue mist. Layers of hills in shades of azure, indigo, and teal faded into the distance. That's why they're called the Blue Ridge, Grace mused.

"I've been thinking about planting grapes to start a vineyard, buy a nice piece of land up here," Dickie said. "I'm through with school."

"Did you ever graduate?" she asked, without believing.

"Heavens no," Dickie said. "I've run out of patience."

She wandered over to the barn stalls to see the horses about to race. Their big warm bodies, well curried, smelled of careful breeding and grooming. Jared and his friends were young aristocrats, heirs of Richmond's finest families. They weren't so much dumb as lazy. At twenty-three and twenty-four, they still lived in their parents' houses and partied weekends at family beach cottages and country places. Dickie Grimes had flunked out of three colleges and more prep schools. At least Jared was in business school. He was brighter than any of his friends, but what he wanted most was to blend in. Jared's friends were pleasant bums, but they'd been loyal to each other since kindergarten at St. Christopher's.

Back at the cars, Three Morgan, who was always a little crazy, slipped under the white rail fence onto the steeplechase course. He used to run track in high school but was considerably out of shape. He got a running start from fifty yards, hoping to clear the boxwood obstacle like a steeplechase horse. Three lay sprawled on top of the hedge, wiggled down to his feet, and walked seventy-five yards farther down the track.

From the fence, Jared yelled encouragement, "Way to go, Three."

Three took off his tennis shoes and threw them to the fence, started running, picked up speed, dove head first over the five-foot hedge, and rolled on his shoulder on the grass. He lay there in triumph. Four people at the fence applauded him.

"Hey, Three, better get out of the way. The next race is lining up, and we bet on your horse."

Three had grass stains on the back of his white shirt.

After two more races, Dickie said, "Come on, let's leave before the traffic. Grace, are you going to follow us to the Lindbergs?"

"I know the way," she said.

Five miles west of Orange, the Lindberg house was built in 1780, a three-story, red-brick colonial plantation house on a hill overlooking a floodplain cornfield by the Rapidan River. Mrs. Lindberg lived alone in the big house. When her sons came back on weekends, their friends partied in the guesthouse across the driveway, on the hill with a long porch overlooking a lake and the river. The boys' dates shared bedrooms in the guesthouse, and the guys stayed in a cabin in the apple orchard.

Many nights no one slept much. Before Mr. Lindberg died, Grace had met him late one night. He had invented something like the ball bearing, and his family lived on the royalties from the patent. Behind the bar counter in the guesthouse was a wall full of photographs painted with lacquer. She identified Mr. Lindberg, tall and Nordic, partying with Jared's crowd.

"Last fall a copperhead bit Three at the orchard cabin," Dickie said after dinner. "The venom ate a great gouge of meat in his calf before we got him to the hospital in Culpeper."

"The snake bite didn't chew up his skin," Jared corrected. "It was the antivenom. Hey Grace, be my tennis partner in doubles tomorrow."

He was no athlete, but he always dressed the part, wearing a tennis sweater draped over his shoulders. The navy and maroon stripes around the V-neck, waist, and wrists matched his navy-blue linen pants and set off his pink Lacoste shirt. He was as portly and conservative as a forty-year-old stockbroker, and Grace could beat him in tennis.

"I can't. I'm going to Charlottesville." Jared followed her out to the porch overlooking the lake. They sat in bentwood Adirondack chairs.

He said, "You know, you're screwing up by not taking Tolly's advice to sell your farm." So Jared knew about the dam.

"It's mine," she said, "and I'm going to stop the dam."

"Don't be a fool," he said. "And don't do anything to embarrass us." Jared was drinking bourbon neat.

"Is appearance the only thing important to you?" she said. "I'm going to fight for what I believe in."

"Where are you getting these radical ideas?" Jared asked.

"Good heavens," she said. "I thought Republicans respected private property."

"I'm a Virginia Democrat," he said. "Who are you going to vote for this fall? You know that Mac Hutchinson is opposing Dan Chesterfield for Congress?"

"In Virginia, state Democrats are national Republicans," she said. "Mac is a bright fellow. He was head of his class at Harvard Law."

"Yes, but he's only three years older than me," Jared said. He was jealous or threatened by Richmond boys who went north to college. Tolly had convinced Jared that northern colleges were full of Communists.

"Dan Chesterfield is antediluvian," Grace said. "He hasn't had a new idea since before the flood. At least you must want a representative who has a brain. Old Dan voted against the Environmental Policy Act, against the Endangered Species Act, the Clean Water Act." She was furious that Jared wanted to dictate the way she should vote. Any Richmond man wanted to control his daughter or wife or sister.

"Yes, but Dan represents his constituency," Jared said. "He votes the way Richmond wants. That's why we re-elect him." He smelled of after-shave and bourbon. His hair fell in his eyes.

Grace said, "Wouldn't you rather have someone who understands history and economics well enough to improve our country?" She wanted to voice her own convictions, but she didn't want Jared to cause a scene. "I don't want to argue when you have a chip on your shoulder."

He said, "We don't need civil-rights liberals, messing up our society. So are you going to vote for Mac?"

She said, "You imagine I'm more radical than I really am."

"You sit there smug on a log like Tar Baby. Answer me." Jared's fist shot out and jammed against her jaw. She recoiled, shocked, reached up to feel if her left jawbone had been broken. Jared was shocked too. Maybe he had intended to shadow-punch her, but couldn't judge the distance drunk.

Grace stood up. No one else in the guesthouse had noticed. She wrapped ice from the bar refrigerator in a linen towel to put on her jaw. She didn't want to give Jared the satisfaction of knowing he had hurt her. His taunts were attempts to get her to say "uncle," and she never did.

The noise of people talking and laughing inanely filled the guesthouse. At that moment behind the bar counter, Grace became aware that she had frozen her outrage at Jared inside her. When she stopped feeling emotionally is how she got hurt *physically*: She would end up with a sprained ankle or a huge bruise. That was why she thought she was clumsy. She fell down instead of breaking her reserve.

The ice made her jaw numb. She rolled her jawbone side to side. At least it wasn't broken. She didn't want to be numb inside anymore. She would try to be angry. She went out to the front porch and weighed her options, deciding whether to stay or leave.

Dinah, Dickie's girlfriend, followed Grace outside. "Please come back in," Dinah said. "Jared's all upset. Come tell him it's all right."

"*He's* upset? He hit *me*!" She did let loose her anger. "Why should I take care of Jared's feelings instead of my own?" He hurt her to make himself feel better. She was just as angry with herself that she almost went to comfort him. Grace was not going to coddle his drunken ego.

At eleven, the party would go on all night. She found her new tent that she had pitched below a screen of trees overlooking the lake. At daylight Grace woke with a sore jaw. Long before anyone in the guesthouse was stirring, she slipped in to use the bathroom. Three was sacked out on a couch. As she drove the lane along the lake, Mrs. Lindberg emerged from the water, naked, and pulled on a terrycloth robe. At sixty, Nordic Mrs. Lindberg looked forty and could play a mean game of tennis.

She waved as Grace drove out, "Aren't you staying for the round robin and Bloody Mary's this morning?"

114

17

In Charlottesville, Grace looked up Friends Meeting at a pay phone and called a number for directions. The Meeting House was yellow clapboard with a front porch like the farmhouse. In the big room that filled the first floor, people wore jeans, khaki shorts, India-print skirts—with a casualness that Grace thought odd for church. She sat in a folding metal chair in the back row. She didn't see Sam anywhere.

In the continuing silence she could hear individual watches tick and feared her stomach would gurgle. She wondered when something was going to happen. After fifteen minutes, a slight man with a white goatee stood. Perhaps this was the clerk Chester who called country-dances. He cleared his voice and recited one of Kenneth Boulding's Naylor Sonnets. James Naylor, he said, was a Quaker mystic who rode into a town on a donkey as Jesus had done. Grace caught parts of the poem:

> Can grief be gift, love's gift. . .
> No greater song than this. . .
> That there is joy, greater than Joy can know,
> Through suffering, on the far side of woe.

"Another of Boulding's sonnets comforts me," Chester with the goatee said,

> But as the seed must grow into the tree
> So life is love, and love the end must be.

Grace fidgeted, squirmed, her stomach growled, but no one else noticed. She looked out the window past the edge of the porch at parked cars. She heard voices of children on a playground.

A tiny woman in a red-plaid dress and red Keds stood, "Look in the mirror and see the most destructive animal on earth. Humans are wiping out more species in a hundred years than in all creation. We need to outgrow the idea that we have dominion. All creatures are part of a connected, complicated web."

Wow, Grace thought, the old lady delivered an ecological message.

Her eyes followed the circle of feet at floor level—in sandals, work boots dried with red clay, and running shoes. She looked up at a poster on the opposite wall: "Live Simply That Others May Simply Live." Out another window she saw filigree branches and dogwood blossoms, like the grove of trees up the hollow behind the farm where as a child she had helped Ruby gather herbs.

Wordsworth said the child is father to the man. Grace tried to remember the little girl with pigtails in the orchard. If she could remember her own joy, then maybe she could break through her grief and guilt. Wordsworth wrote, "My heart leaps up when I behold." She mused, The whole point in nature is to be aware. If only I could be more awake. Gratitude swept over her for the woods at the farm and for her love of good books.

When the thin man extended his hand to shake hers, Grace was startled out of her reverie. People in the circle started to introduce themselves, but she suddenly felt shy and slipped out.

She walked across the University grounds to the Environmental Sciences department in Clark Hall to find Sam. The marble entry led to a central hall with a solarium roof two stories high. Along the walls, rocks filled glass cases like a jewelry store. The long walls were covered with murals of classical Greek figures, wrapped in vibrant-color sheets. Men and women in small-group conversations leaned against marble columns and lounged on steps at the marketplace. Grace turned to survey much the same arrangement of figures on the opposite wall, except—she was startled to see—the men were undraped, all naked. She checked if anyone noticed her astonishment. No one watched her take a second look at the men's anatomy.

Clark Hall used to house the University Law School. In the arched doorway a note explained the legal themes of the murals. On the east wall, a clothed Moses delivered stone tablets, representing the law of the individual. The west wall's naked bodies

116

depicted a trial from the *Iliad* over the blood-price of a slain man. Here law settled disputes, weighing the interests of groups over individuals. So frequently, she mused, the freedoms of the self-sufficient farmers in McDowell suffer when measured against benefits to the whole system.

Grace did not find Sam in his lab. If he wasn't home, she'd drive back to the farm. By the library door she found a phone, dialed his number, and he answered, "Come on over."

"Celebrate," she proclaimed. "I just graduated from high school."

Ben rented one big room in the basement of a widow's shingled ranch house, close enough so he could cycle to class. Dim light came in from the windows at ground level, but he spent little time there except to sleep. For lunch, Sam cut up an apple and a banana, mixed them with yogurt, and sprinkled in wheat germ and sesame seeds. What is he? she thought—a bird? With no breakfast, Grace needed to eat, but did not ask for more.

"I went to Quaker Meeting this morning. I thought you might be there." She did not mention the nude murals in Clark Hall.

"Pete and I paddled a creek with enough water only in the spring. Soon we will have run all the rivers in Virginia together. How did you like the silence at Meeting?" She nodded. Sam said, "Hey look, do you mind if I work half an hour? Grades are due tomorrow, and I have to correct a pile of exams. More work-study."

Carrying dishes from the table to the sink, Grace couldn't help thinking that he had paddled first and put off grading until the last minute. She did not admit that she had procrastinated her own Wordsworth paper until the deadline. Pachelbel's Canon in D was on the radio. She looked over to Sam settling at his desk. She was up to her elbows in dishwater. Single tears welled up in her eyes, and she reached to wipe them. When she looked up, Sam was watching her.

He asked, "What's the story?"

117

"Nothing," Grace said, then loosened up, "Last night Jared hit me. I thought he had broken my left jaw."

"Why on earth?" he said.

"Over some political argument that I wouldn't argue with him."

"Gee. Are you all right?" he asked.

Grace nodded and dried her hands. She browsed bookshelves and pulled out Aldo Leopold's *A Sand County Almanac* to read. On the concrete patio she lay on a deck chair to read. Leopold had restored an old farm in Wisconsin, much as Grace was learning the rhythms of her father's farm.

After an hour, Sam came to the patio door and said, "Half done. Want a backrub?"

She said, "Sure."

He said, "Roll over on your stomach." Through her T-shirt Sam kneaded the muscles in her neck and shoulders. He pushed her skin under the bone in each shoulder blade and rolled his knuckles along her ribs.

"Like a lump of dough," he said.

"Bread baking comes in handy," Grace said. "Where did you learn this?"

"From my mother. She used to refrigerate alcohol for backrubs in the summer when we had no air-conditioning."

With two fingers he followed the indentation down her spine from her neck to her waist, three times with more pressure. Then he pulled each arm down along her side, squeezed her palms, and pulled fingers longer at each joint. He stopped and was quiet.

"Thanks," she said. "Your turn."

"Rain check," he said. "You know, Grace, you're a little too young. I'm too busy . . . ."

"Then it's time for me to drive back," she said. "I miss Ruby and the animals. I want to wake up in time for the milking."

"Congratulations on graduating," Sam said. "Will I see you at the square dance?"

18

Folks in McDowell County gathered for a square dance in the Sweetgum Elementary School cafeteria on the first Friday night every month. Grace carried Ruby's butterscotch pies heaped with whipped cream to the dessert table. Sam had not shown up for dinner before the dance, so she and Ruby carpooled with Amos, Harry, and Clara. People from other valleys came to speak to Ruby, and she introduced them to Grace. Millie Dorset sat next to Ruby, and Charlie carried his mandolin case to join the band. At the piano on stage was Elsie Moyers, the school music teacher. Farley Dodge tuned a fiddle.

"Farley's part Indian, you know," Ruby said. "He claims he's Melungeon, but nobody knows who the Melungeon were or where they came from. One of his grandfathers was a freed slave who had married an Indian princess, descendant of Cornstalk, the warrior who led massacres."

The dance caller, Butler Mizner from Churchville in Augusta County, spoke up, "Everyone grab a partner, young and old. Get in a big circle."

In a smaller brace Ruby could put weight on her leg, but she would not dance. Next to Ruby, Sally Bee Pollock was holding her newborn son, born the weekend before.

"We named him Timothy Thomas, after Waller's brother and his father. Mr. Pollock was named Thomas just like your father. I thought you'd like that." Sally Bee unfolded the blanket from his fat feet. "He looks like a little wrestler."

"Sally Bee, he's handsome," Grace touched the soft skin of his feet. "Mr. T."

"Grace, I want to ask: will you be Timmy's godmother. He'll be christened in a week."

"Wow, Sally, I'm honored. May I hold him?"

"Wait until he's asleep so he doesn't cry. You go dance right now."

Butler Mizner called again for a circle. Grace recognized Anglebergers, Millers, Puffenbargers, Curries, Clines, Browns, and Conways. Women's colorful calico dresses had full skirts for twirling. About half wore crinolines. The men wore western shirts with pearl snap buttons and long sleeves; some had small towels on their belts to wipe sweaty hands. Amos pulled Grace to the dance floor.

"I don't know how," she said.

"You know your left from your right," Amos said. "You can walk in time to music. Hold your hands up so we can pull you through."

The caller gave instructions for a circle mixer dance. "Ladies on the gent's right. Circle left, circle back clickety-clack." As the music started, he kept calling the moves, "Everybody to the center with a great big shout, then back up, come on out. Circle four. Dos y dos your corner."

The rhythm of the music swept Grace into the dance, as piano chords thumped a steady beat and Farley's fiddle wove the fabric of melodies. Charlie's mandolin strumming filled in a beat or so behind.

"Dive for the oyster, dig for the clam." Farmers' strong hands on her waist pushed Grace where she was supposed to go.

When the band stopped, Butler Mizner said, "Square up," and then, "We need two more couples in the back of the room." Before she could sit next to Ruby, Amos led Grace into a square with Esther and Enoch Conway on their right. To the left of Amos, Punch Breedlove, who ran the Feed Store in Jackson, stood with his twelve-year-old daughter; his wife, Agnes, and their fifteen-year-old son were across the square. Nobody would ever get a teenage boy in Richmond up dancing with his mother, Grace thought. She took a second look: Agnes Breedlove was blind.

"Allemande left your corner. Grand right and left," sang Butler in a crisp cadence. When Grace did not know what to do, the men pulled her in a circle, right hand over left hand. Just as Enoch and Amos pulled Grace, a beginner, through the dance,

Agnes Breedlove's husband as her corner and her son as her partner led the smiling blind woman.

The wooden floor rang as feet thumped in unison with the eight-beat rhythm. The fiddle and piano and mandolin swept Grace along. She grinned like Agnes Breedlove.

"Listen to the fiddle, head couples swing in the middle."

Grace felt she would fly off her feet with the centrifugal force, but Amos held on tight as he whisked her in a dizzy swing. Amos was spindly and awkward-looking, but on the dance floor, with elbows and knees akimbo, he moved with suave assurance. He danced for the joy of moving, not for any appearance.

When the music stopped, Butler said, "Bow to your partner, bow to your corner." Amos and Enoch bowed and thanked her, and Amos went to ask Millie Dorset to dance. As people found new partners, a thirteen-year-old Puffenbarger boy asked Grace to dance. At the break, people drank cider, ate cupcakes and sliced peaches. They milled around laughing and chatting.

Back on stage alone, Farley sawed his fiddle, and the floor cleared for free-style cloggers. Amos and several others walked out on the floor. Amos looked at Farley, without speaking. Farley nodded back and grinned. In syncopation, Amos shuffled on the balls of his feet and stomped on his heels, as if his legs dangled loose from his knees.

Amos called, "Come on, Grace, let me show you how."

She copied the basic shuffle-back step, as Amos lifted his knees high, doubled his beat in intricate nonchalance, stepped one foot behind the other in a grapevine figure. Grace laughed and sat down. As Farley accelerated his pace, other cloggers thinned out until Amos was step-dancing alone to faster and faster music. The crowd clapped in time. Amos was getting winded, but would not stop before Farley.

"Who's gonna win this duel?" Harry asked Ruby.

"Like schoolboys showing off, both of them," Ruby answered.

Finally Amos had to concede. Everybody applauded for him

and for Farley. On stage Farley bowed to Amos, and Amos bowed back.

Back on stage, Butler called for new squares to form. Grace sat next to Ruby who rocked and bobbed baby Tim while Sally Bee and Waller danced. Almost three, Loretta slept on a quilt under the dessert table, tucked away safe from dancing feet.

Ruby said, "You know, I took care of you when you were this size." Grace nodded in quiet acceptance. "Here," Ruby said, "you hold Tim. You're his godmother, just like I'm yours."

Grace clasped the warm bundle gingerly and looked at his squeezed-up features, as she listened to Ruby tell a story to several ladies sitting with her. "An old hermit used to live halfway up Bluff Mountain. He was a Covenanter and a Presbyterian, but he never went to church. He did penance like a monk. He believed that he would never die and that if he climbed to the top of the Bluff, he would ascend to his God like Elijah." She coughed. Ruby was a minister to her community, more than the circuit preacher who did not live among them.

"Well, he lived to a ripe good age," Ruby said. "His white hair covered his shoulders, and his beard reached nearly to his waist. He did disappear when he was about eighty. They found not a trace of him and supposed he climbed the hill and ascended to his God." Ruby's circle of listeners was quiet while she took a long draft of sweet cider.

"With this old leg feeling stronger, I look forward to climbing the hill again. A mountain is a place where a person might meet her God. There is such divinity and power on a mountain, so grand and restful. When I am weary and my mind tires, I go in spirit to the top of a hill and rest, like the old hermit."

Grace marveled at the simplicity of Ruby's faith. Sally Bee came back after the next dance to check on the baby; Ruby took Tim and sent them both off to dance.

"Ruby, I'm tired from all-nighters rocking Timmy," Sally protested.

"You dance when you get a chance, child," Ruby said.

As Grace danced the next set with Enoch Conway, she saw Sam walk on the stage, arriving late, open his banjo case, lean his head over to tune the strings, and then join the band. He wore a horribly gaudy purple-and-green flowered shirt. She expected Sam to dance with her, but he walked down between squares only to ask, "Hey, Grace, are you ready to drum up some support for a scenic river?"

"Good to see you," she said. "I'm scared to talk on stage alone. Why are you so late?"

"Dodging woolly worms, crawling all over the road this early," he said. "Gonna be a cold winter. Naw, I got a late start because I've got a new idea from looking at topographic maps. Maybe I really can find an endangered species. I'm going to check out a geological theory of stream piracy." As he turned, Sam added, "Save the last waltz for me. I'll tell Butler to announce you."

At the next break, Sam adjusted the microphone to fit Grace and then went to sit with Ruby. Grace spoke quietly to the dancers. "I was born here, and raised downstate, but I plan to settle in McDowell on my family's farm. I have come as an outsider, and you welcome me back. But just as soon as I get home, the power company says it will flood our land. I want to know who will help me stop the dam."

Grace looked around to see if anybody eating pie agreed with her or not. She looked back at Sam next to Ruby; he grinned and Ruby nodded.

Grace cleared her throat and spoke louder, "I feel grief and anger. Cities that use too much electricity like Dayton and Detroit want to flood our farms in Virginia, where we use hardly any electricity at all. They will string power lines across three states. We've got to tell legislators in Richmond that our family land is sacred. How many generations of your family have lived on your land? For how long?"

Voices rang out big numbers—"One hundred years." "Two centuries." Grace tried to read expressions in the sea of faces.

She said, "We need the attention of newspapers. If we stand

together, the state will hear our voices. One way we can stop the dam is for the state to declare Jack Creek a scenic river. Other Virginians support our right to protect our farms, because they like wild clean rivers, because Jack Creek is beautiful. With a scenic river, we can still farm our land and keep on cutting timber. A scenic river is the best way because we won't have to leave our land. I will try to answer your questions."

No one started to speak, but Grace had planted a few questions. Harry Benton asked, "Will the federal government zone my land so I can't build on it?"

"No sir, only our local county government can pass any zoning. Most likely, one rule will be a floodplain building setback, so many feet from the river."

Creed Huffman asked, "Grace, will the state government look over my shoulder at what I do?"

"No, Creed. You can paint your house pink or pave your driveway." He chuckled.

"Does this river protection hurt our job prospects?" Waller Pollock spoke up. "Dam construction will give us jobs."

"From what I understand, Waller, the power company will import union labor from up north; the dam will hire very few local workers to build it, and none to run it. Now, we do earn money from tourism. If we keep our scenic river, fishermen and hikers will buy food, gas, bait, and lodging."

"Does that mean outsiders will trespass on our land and bring in crime?" Punch Breedlove asked.

"No sir. Your land is still your private land."

"Will this scenic-river plan stop the dam that will flood my land?" asked Millie Dorset.

"Yes ma'am. That's what I want to do. Stop the dam, and keep the creek. We have a lot to celebrate. I invite you all to a Jack Creek festival on Ruby's farm on July 14." Grace thought it appropriate to rebel against authority on the day the French Revolution started. Bastille Day also happened to be her eighteenth birthday, when she would own the farm.

124

As Grace walked back toward Ruby and Sam, people encouraged her that she was not alone opposing the dam.

Sam played his banjo for the last set of squares, then found Grace for the waltz. He said, "You spoke really well." Ben was not a smooth dancer, but she felt good dancing with someone her height, instead of straining her neck to look up at Amos.

Ruby rode home with the Bentons. In his bus on the way back to the farm, Grace prompted Sam, "Tell me about your stream piracy. Can we lift up Jack Creek and hide it until the power company forgets it?"

"No, this piracy took place after the sea receded at the end of the Mississippian Age, about 340 million years ago. Back then, the James and the Roanoke rivers originated on the east slope of the Blue Ridge. West of the Blue Ridge, the Teays River, which is now the New, flowed north and west. North of the Teays was the Potomac, and south was the Tennessee. In the early Pennsylvanian era . . . ."

"Whoa, Sam, slow down," Grace said. "I forget my geology lesson."

"Oh yeah, the Pennsylvanian was 300 million years ago," he added. "First the Roanoke River eroded west across the scarp of the Blue Ridge and pirated streams from the Teays. Then in Wisconsin time, the James broke a water gap through the Blue Ridge at Glasgow and captured what the Roanoke had stolen."

"How can you prove that?" Grace asked.

"Scientists can verify that streams used to be in the same river system by finding twin species unique to those places."

"How does that help us?" she asked.

"Well, looking at the topo map, I see that headwaters of the James and of the Potomac start along the same ridge just at the head of Jack Creek Valley. I can prove that the James stole the Potomac, if I can find some distinctive endangered species in the headwaters of both rivers."

"Couldn't some person or a bird carry fish between rivers?"

"Possibly. I'll keep a look on hybrid speciation in gene pools of separate river systems. Come over to West Virginia and help me with my fieldwork."

"I can't miss Sally Bee's baby christening next Sunday. I'm the godmother." She was proud Sally had asked her. Grace thought, at least if she never had her own children, or waited another ten or twenty years, she could help raise Sally Bee's babies, as Ruby had raised her.

19

In West Virginia streams, over the ridge west of the farm, Sam was searching for distinctive species similar to those in Jack Creek. If he could prove his theory about stream capture, maybe West Virginia would convince Virginia to protect Jack Creek. If he could find an endangered species, the new federal law would stop the dam.

On Straight Fork and Laurel Fork, parallel tributaries of the north fork of the south branch of the Potomac, Grace helped Sam collect insects. At six stops where the road intersected the streams, they waded a hundred yards. She held a canvas-and-mesh net on a D-shaped ring downstream as he lifted bread-loaf-sized stones, rubbed their bottoms, and stirred up sediment so the current carried tiny aquatic insects into the net. They rolled over small rocks to pick insect larvae that looked to her like tiny wiggly threads and popped them into little glass bottles of alcohol, marked for each stop.

"Cranefly, mayfly, caddisfly, stonefly," Sam catalogued the larvae. "Indicators of pristine water quality, but no rare species."

Hot and sunny, with a stainless blue sky, it was a good day to wade wet in cut-off jeans and tennis shoes, moving downstream with the brisk current.

"Getting wet is what you mean by groundtruthing," she said. She was learning to distinguish each species. "Working in the field is certainly more satisfying than sitting at a desk. Philosophers should catch their ideas outside, instead of stewing brain juice in libraries."

Grace scuffed her ankles and knees, slipped and tumbled, so that she was all wet. "Good thing the water's warming. How do you stay dry in the winter?"

"Neoprene waders," he answered, "but trout like cold water."

She saw it would be easy in a strong current to pin an ankle under the rocks. "Aren't you nervous, Sam, when you work alone wading the river?"

"There's a certain amount of risk I can take with another person along that I can't take alone," he said. "In fording streams, to avoid the risk of a twisted ankle teetering on slippery rocks, I'd rather get my feet wet wading. If there's nobody to go for help, I can't break my ankle. Overconfidence is more dangerous than inexperience. Alone I'm even more safety conscious."

At the head of Laurel Fork on the ridgetop of National Forest land, where rhododendron bushes, red spruce, and hemlock boughs completely shaded the narrow fast stream, the water temperature was 60 degrees, the dissolved oxygen was high, and they found the most different species and individual insects. Further downstream on Straight Fork where more sunlight could warm the water through the higher canopy of oak trees and where the rocks were bigger, there were fewer species of insects. At their last sampling station just above Seneca Creek, the boulders in the streambed were almost too big to turn over, and they disturbed almost no insects on the bottom.

Sam discovered no insects more rare than he usually sampled, so he consulted taxonomic books for mussels and fish. He narrowed his search to a small family of neon-color guppies that burrow in the gravel.

He announced, "I'll bet I can find a red-bellied mountain dace or a yellow-sided dace. Thoreau said he was more likely to see a certain flower if he pictured what he was looking for."

After wading all day they ate spaghetti for supper at a café in Judy Gap. Sam drove up a steep dirt road to a small clearing facing Seneca Rocks just in time to watch the sunset. Rose-orange wisps of cloud faded over shadowed folds of hills gradually turning darker shades of green. While Sam tuned his banjo on a rock overlook, Grace pitched her new green tent.

She asked, "Hey, Sam, what do you see as your future?"

"Science," he said. "There's always more to know about how a river works. Maybe, if we see how natural communities work, we can learn how humans can get along."

128

"How about personal goals? What do you want out of life?"

"Someday somebody I love will love me back. I want to settle with a person, but not one place. I can't promise a white picket fence." The sky went mauve before darkness.

"Oh Sam, I don't see anybody putting up with me." Grace wanted somebody special too. Sam wasn't proper, and he wasn't perfect. She went into the tent to undress and lay down to sleep on a pad, listening to his banjo.

In the tent Grace sat bolt upright after a dream to check her value system. In her dream camping on top of Seneca, Will arrived in Richmond from London to court her. She took him to a party at Three Morgan's lake in Midlothian. She pictured Dickie and Dinah diving off the pier to swim to the float, Jared stirring the black iron cauldron of Brunswick Stew, which called for corn, tomatoes, lima beans, and squirrel. When she drove Will to the bus station on his way back north, he asked her, "Come north and live with me."

In her dream, she said no. After college she'd marry the man first in her graduate class, or in law school, so she could get the second highest grades. There was bound to be some guy smarter than she was. She would not drop out, as Sally Bee had left high school. After she got married, she would delay babies until she finished her PhD. Grace never saw any further than that. Graduate school and work seemed to fit into her plans, but she was not sure yet about marriage and babies.

Grace woke early and walked down the cliff path to the crossroad store for sweet rolls and hot brewed coffee to bring Sam, who was still sleeping inside the bus.

At the door of the general store a fellow in a tan leather jacket spoke to her. "You're Jared's sister, aren't you? I went to school with him. I'm Hugh Westwood." He shook her hand. He caught her attention in some way that was intellect, chemistry, or risk. Despite her resolve not to value material things, his leather jacket and defined features touched Grace as classy.

"Want a cup of coffee?" Hugh asked. By the curb she noticed a bright blue Porsche with the top down.

"No, I have to meet a friend," she said, wary because this guy Hugh was too charming. "Well, okay."

Grace talked with him over coffee for an hour. Hugh taught French at a private girls-school near Washington. He asked her to spend the day with him, and she said no. Hugh quoted in French from St. Exupéry's *The Little Prince*. "'*On risque de pleurer si on se laisse apprivoiser.*' You're spooked just like the little fox who refused to be tamed for fear of crying."

Walking uphill from the crossroads, Grace could see vibrant parkas of climbers on the cliff face of Seneca Rocks. At a distance, they were the size of insects linked by threads that were climbing ropes. When she was gone, Sam had awakened and did not know where she was. He ran downhill, had asked for her in the store, and the storekeeper had not seen her. When Grace climbed the path with his coffee and rolls, she encountered him running into town the second time.

"Where on earth have you been?" Sam demanded.

"I'm sorry. I ran into a friend of Jared's at the store, and we started talking."

"I thought that you might have fallen." He sounded angry and protective like a parent. His concern soured into sullenness as they climbed the hill. "You know, you were really inconsiderate."

Grace felt trapped.

"You won't trust anybody else," he said. "You can't even trust yourself."

The idea of leaving Sam and driving home with Hugh had scared Grace. She didn't like facing that she could control her own destiny. She didn't want choice but inevitability. Her most difficult decision, so far, had been in tenth grade when she chose to play hockey, with the jocks, instead of being a cheerleader, with the daters. She couldn't decide where to go to college. Eleanor had said she would pay for a Virginia woman's school—Sweet Briar, Hollins, Mary Baldwin, or Randolph Macon, so her daughter could keep her southern graces.

Crossroads: Here was another choice Grace shrugged off.

She could have left with Hugh. Would she ever leave Sam again? Out of the blue she said, "Sam, how do I know if we ever get married that I won't walk out someday? When I'm thirty-five and we have three kids, I might drive to the grocery store some morning and never come back." That possibility scared her, and it must have scared him too. She was worried she could walk away from children as her mother had done.

"I don't want to be a bad mother like Eleanor," she told Sam. "I don't want to abandon anyone or be abandoned again."

"Well, settle down, Grace, we've got work to do," he mumbled as they packed the bus. After they had scouted Seneca Creek and South Fork until three, they drove up the steep nine-mile approach road to Dolly Sods, a 4,000-foot plateau.

"I think I can, I think I can," he reminded the old VW, shifting into second gear and then first. "You got to see Dolly Sods. The National Forest just declared it a wilderness area."

At the parking area, to divide weight between their two packs, Grace carried her new tent and Sam carried its poles. They planned to stay overnight, but had enough food for three days. She was breaking in her new pack and hiking boots as well.

"Aren't you the fashionable backpacker?" His sarcasm surprised her. Was he jealous she could afford new gear? She had bought it to go camping with him.

He said, "The big trees here were all cut in the timber boom in 1900. Used to be red spruce twelve-feet diameter, ninety feet tall. The Nature Conservancy bought the coal-mining rights for fifteen million dollars, or this land all could have been open-pit mining."

Grace read the contours on the topo map as they followed a trail four miles. They set up camp by a creek under a hillside covered with blueberry bushes. They planned to pick blueberries for Ruby to make pies for the Jack Creek festival in two weeks. For supper, Sam heated a can of Dinty Moore beef stew on his gas stove.

The sun set at nine. "That's Orion," Grace pointed out a star. "I always recognize the three stars of his belt." She wondered if

Sam would share the small tent since no rain was forecast, but he rolled his sleeping bag on a mat outside.

He said, "Let's find a clearing to see more stars."

Walking along the creekbank in the dark, they could hear riffles beside them. Abruptly Sam stepped off the bank, pulling her along. It was a bigger drop than he expected. In mid-air Grace marveled how long it took before she hit ground. He landed on his feet on the rocks, five or six feet down. Pulled off balance, she landed on her left side and let out a scream.

"Grace, are you okay?" he asked.

"I don't know." She was scared she was crippled. She shrugged her shoulder. "Ow ow." Her left-side muscle was stretched or torn. "I really hurt."

"Can you stand up?" Sam leaned over her.

"Not yet." She could move her arms and legs without pain. She was bruised but not broken. "I'm okay." But she blamed him for leaping off in the dark without looking, without knowing the distance, without telling her. When she caught her breath, Sam helped her limp to the tent.

"Let me see." He pressed the bones in her side. "You didn't break anything. Your side muscle is bruised. We'll see how you feel in the morning."

In the morning Grace did not want to get up, and she did not want to talk to Sam. She didn't trust his judgment. Could she ever put her welfare into someone else's hands?

"Breakfast in bed," he announced. He appeared in the door of the tent with Bisquick pancakes full of blueberries.

She leaned her weight on one elbow. "Please take me to a hospital for an x-ray."

"A doctor would tell you to take it easy. You can't hobble out four miles today anyway, even if I do carry your pack. We'll stay another day, until you can walk out, and I'll carry all the weight."

"I'll end up a hunch-backed dwarf like Quasimodo," she moaned.

Sam arranged her camping mat and purple sleeping bag

against a rock so Grace was comfortable in the sun. "You're exaggerating. Lie still."

"I'm out of commission for tennis season. No way to toss the ball to serve."

"You're not playing much tennis when you work on the farm." He poured another pile of blueberries into her bowl. "Sing to me."

"I can't breathe deep enough with my side hurting."

"Stick out your tongue." By this time Sam and Grace both had blue tongues.

Together they alternated in a litany: "Blueberry pie, blueberry cobbler, blueberry ice cream, blueberry milkshakes, blueberry muffins, blueberry mousse."

"Blueberry moose?" he laughed.

When Sam wandered off filling a bucket, Grace warned as a joke, "Watch out for the bears. You're picking on their turf."

"There's plenty to share," he called back, and she knew Sam could make friends with a bear. Exasperated with her injury, she couldn't help but like him. Grace looked closely at the tiny stunted spruce trees growing on the heather. On the high plateau, spruce trees dwarfed by exposure to cold wind were shorter than wild flowers. She hummed tunes with an Irish lilt.

"Dolly Sods smells like the northern woods," she said, when Sam approached.

"That's because the climate at 4,000 feet is more like Canada—1,600 miles north—than West Virginia. Hey, I'm sorry about your back. I was impetuous."

"No joke. I should heal. I'm still less afraid of risks in nature than in cities. At the farm I have to keep an eye out for rattlesnakes, but I don't worry when I walk half a mile to Sally Bee's in pitch black. In Richmond, Tolly warns me not to walk in dark and lonely places. Now I want to shoot out city streetlights, because I can't see the stars."

"That reminds me," he said. "A friend of mine, Buck Bond, director of Oregon Outward Bound, told this story:

133

"At the end of a month trip, kids on Outward Bound take three-day solos to test their 'survival' skills. As a rule, inner-city kids are less comfortable in the wilds. Without bright lights and traffic noise, people from the city get scared. So, one time, there were three inner-city teenagers from Newark, New Jersey, on scholarship. After Buck placed each kid at a one-acre solo site, these three boys returned to Buck's campsite just at dark, and they slept there next to him. The next morning he took the boys back to their own solo fields. The second night, two boys returned to Buck's campsite.

"On the third day, Buck walked to the alpine meadow with exquisite wildflowers and a burbling brook where he had left the third kid. The boy was sitting in the same spot in the same position as two days before. Buck sat down next to him. The boy didn't speak, so Buck picked up the little notebook where the boy was supposed to keep a journal. In the empty book he found one line, 'Damn stream acts like it owns the place.'"

"Great story," Grace said. "This stream sure does own Dolly Sods."

"Are you angry with me?"

"Yes." But she couldn't be stern.

Sam wanted to make peace. "We'll get along better if you tell me when you're mad, instead of moping. Yell at me a little," he said, and Grace laughed.

When Grace got back to the farm after camping, there was a letter from Will: "Your cards to Princeton finally caught up to me. I'm in Zurich on a UN internship for six months. If you're back in Europe before September, I'd like to see you."

Grace was tempted to fly to Switzerland, but she had a river festival to supervise on Bastille Day.

20

With her sore back slowing her down, Grace told Ruby, "I can't get it all done in time. My left side hurts. I can't lift anything. We'll have to cancel the festival."

"Nonsense," Ruby said. "You'll just have to ask for help the way I did when I broke my leg. Delegate jobs to everyone else in the valley. Besides, the more people contribute, the more they'll feel part of defending the creek." Grace never ceased to marvel at Ruby's wisdom.

Her own genius was concentration; Grace threw her body at a job, often getting bruised in the process. In southern society, double-whammy either way, she tried to be accepted for her toughness instead of her intelligence. She reminded herself that Rachel Carson got so tired doing science in a marsh all day that her illustrator used to carry her ashore. Margaret Mead got carried up a Samoan mountain on her first anthropology field trip, even if she did invent her case studies. These bright women were determined to keep working, but not too proud for some physical help.

Grace did not know how to be gentle with herself. From Eleanor, she had learned to be competitive. When she had moved to West End Richmond, she felt she did not belong at the private school or the Country Club pool. In high school she got the highest grades, but successful girls were blonde, daters or debutantes, and she was not blonde. She refused when Eleanor wanted to schedule a coming-out party into Richmond society after her first year of college. At her father's farm, nobody cared if she dressed fashionably. Grace felt she belonged in McDowell County.

Farley was helping haul chairs. Ruby had told him to bring more herbal liniment. "I'm not the only one laid up. Grace is moping that her back still hurts," Ruby told him. She rubbed some of Farley's liniment on Grace's back.

"Time and patience cure," Farley said. "Grace, you're sure like Ruby if you aim to heal without spending the time you're meant to sit and think. If you sing your new songs to Ruby, the music will mend both of you."

Farley was canny to guess Grace was writing songs. She drank a cup of his magic spring water.

Friday, the day before the river festival, while shelling peas in the shade on the front porch, Grace watched Creed Huffman mow an extra field for parking cars. With neighbors scurrying around, she had nothing to do. Rather than tell people what needed to be done, she nodded at their good ideas and listened to her own daydreaming.

The creek meant so many things, lovely and fearful. As a child she had followed her father when he went fishing, and they watched otters play. The creek could be smiling and gentle, or full of fury when it flooded. High water and low, flood and drought, the creek flowed through the valley. The festival celebrated the spirit they would lose if the power company built the dam. Resting her back on the porch, enforcing patience, Grace re-read her father's poems that captured the spirit of the creek, the woods, plants and critters, and cooperating neighbors.

Grace doubted she had enough wisdom to teach anyone anything. She was so young and awkward she could not speak from her own wisdom, as Ruby could—in her simple faith and real-life experience. Who would listen to her? All Grace could hope to do was point out how much beauty there is in the world, the way Amos pointed at useful plants so she could find them herself, and the way Sam showed her intricate insects. The planet seemed to have wisdom in the way animals fit together in an ecosystem. If she could describe the beauty she saw in the valley, maybe people could see for themselves.

But who was she to write about the creek? Wasn't she presumptuous to come back and tell these people? Grace decided to consult the experts. She called all the old ladies along the creek to tell stories under a tent at the festival.

On July 14, Boy Scouts directed traffic, and Enoch Conway

drove a shuttle bus for people who parked down at the churchyard. Jared arrived in his green MG with his Polaroid and twenty boxes of film. To benefit the scenic-river fund-raising, he was going to take pictures of families as Indians and pioneers, sticking their heads through holes in a board painted by the McDowell High School drama club.

"If you want to raise money," Jared advised, "mark off that high pasture in a grid with lime like a football field. Put a cow in the pasture. It's a lottery to see whose grid gets a meadow muffin first."

"Oh Jared, I don't want to offend anyone," Grace protested.

"Sounds like a great idea," said Ruby. "A barnyard cakewalk." Grace was surprised Ruby, too, was susceptible to his flattery.

"Sell chances for five dollars," he said.

"Too much around here, Jared," Ruby bantered. "Twenty-five or fifty cents. Boy, you'll look foolish in those city clothes leading a cow."

He was wearing blue seersucker suit pants. Accordingly, Jared soon re-appeared in a weathered pair of Levis. Ruby went off to the barn to fetch a bag of lime and a cow from the pasture, and a Puffenbarger boy helped Jared mark squares in the field with a hand-pushed seed spreader.

Saturday morning, before everything seemed ready, suddenly locals and tourists began arriving at ten a.m. for the festival. Grace was happier than the auction day when she came home three months earlier. On tables in the shade were crafts for sale to raise money to stop the dam—Martha Huffman's white porcelain plates painted with sweet peas and wild roses, Carolyn Angleberger's apple-head dolls in gingham aprons, and Fred Swope's fine bird carvings that Amos had taught him to make. People bought raffle tickets for one of Charlie Dorset's fine Windsor chairs and a curly-maple dulcimer from Farley. Girl Scouts had organized the baking for a Cake Walk. Fathers were bound to bid on their daughters' cakes, if no one else did.

Stirring a black cauldron, Clara and Harry Benton were

making apple butter. In her sugaring shack Ruby explained how she tapped her maple trees in the spring for sap and boiled the juice in her vats. She displayed her tree plugs, buckets, stove, and her healing leg.

Amos offered samples from his display of edible plants: "Mullein is Indian tobacco to smoke. Jewelweed, or touch-me-not, cures poison-ivy rash. Brew bergamot as tea. If you're hungry out of doors, eat the root of Queen Anne's lace. It's the cousin of the domestic carrot and smells like one, but beware, because Queen Anne's lace looks like water hemlock, which is the poison Socrates drank. Don't eat roots unless you can tell the difference." Amos picked up each plant as illustration. "Grind up chicory root for coffee. Chew wintergreen or sassafras root for a backwoods toothbrush."

Sally Bee tended the table of jams and pickles for sale. Timmy was riding in a fancy fabric baby-sling that Grace had given her. Waller carried Loretta on his shoulders touring the booths.

Fly-casting in the creek, all dressed in his Orvis finery, was Bill Kelly, the real-estate salesman from Jackson. To kids, he gave out fishing poles made from broomsticks with string and hooks attached. "First one to catch a fish wins a prize," Kelly announced to boys and girls. Several ladies in folding chairs settled to baitfish, carrying worms in red tin coffee cans.

Displayed in a big garment box with cellophane on top were fishing flies Grace's father had tied, with delicate feathers in gray and brown. Sam had matched them to the insects he caught in the creek. Dennis Schaeffer, the professor, brought boxes of feathers, thread, and tiny hooks to give fly-tying lessons. Grace expected more of his puns when she stopped to say hello. "Birds of a feather," he started, and she smiled to please him.

To give boat rides, Sam had recruited members of the state canoe-cruising club. Pete Steer, his paddling buddy, drove a mini-bus that hauled a trailer with eight boats. Luckily, it had rained that week, so Jack Creek was not a rock garden. Whoever wanted to see the stretch of river that would be flooded could ride in the bow of a canoe as a passenger. Sam and his paddling crew were especially careful not to dump Millie and other ladies in their cotton dresses.

"Why, I've lived here my whole life, and I never before took a ride on that creek," said Millie. "Who would know how pretty it is? Around the bend, in that shady canyon, I felt I could be miles away from our cow pasture."

Everyone Grace knew in the valley was doing some job for the festival—Amos, the Bentons, Creed, Sally Bee, even Bill Kelly. With everything running smoothly, she settled to listen to Emily Puffenbarger, the retired librarian, at the storytelling tent, donated by the Jackson Funeral Home.

Grace prayed, "Don't ever let me leave where people talk like this—dialect or accent, idioms and images. But more important, mountain people talk from their hearts." She felt the power of her neighbors working together.

Next to the storytellers, a circle of little girls and their grandmothers sewed together a quilt top and backing to raffle off. On the stage, which was a big old wagon with hay bales as steps, twelve Sweetgum School children performed a play about original settlers in the county. The crowd applauded and asked them to repeat the play right away, only slower and a little louder. After an encore, in a white shirt that stayed stiff fresh all day in the sun, Farley played his fiddle in jigs and reels. His dark skin gleamed almost blue against his white-starched collar.

Bill Kelly spoke to Grace, "Farley is so good, he should enter the fiddle contest at Galax."

Helen Brown announced Emily's cousin from West Virginia as the winner of the quilt raffle. A woman from Staunton had the ticket for Charlie's Windsor chair, and a girl from Jackson won Farley's dulcimer; he said he'd give her lessons. A family prize went to the Anglebergers for five generations present—a great-great-grandfather of eighty-four and a new baby, three months.

TV cameras from Staunton and Charlottesville filmed kids sliding like otters down the muddy bank and made the storytellers fluttery and self-conscious. A reporter from the Richmond newspaper rode in the bow of Sam's canoe, while he explained the special pristine ecological value of Jack Creek. On Sunday morning, the state of Virginia would read about the conflict in Jack Creek of small landholders versus the Goliath power company—with a full page of pictures.

On the haywagon stage Farley announced Grace would sing Jean Ritchie's coal-mining protest song. She changed the place name from Kentucky. With her heart pounding, Grace climbed the hay bales.

I come from the mountains, Jack Creek is my home,
Where the wild deer and black bear so lately did roam;
By the cool rushing waterfall the wildflowers dream,
And through every green valley, there runs a clear stream.
Now there's scenes of destruction on every hand
And only black waters run down through my land.
Sad scenes of destruction on every hand,
Black waters, black waters, rise over my land.

The crowd applauded. "Well, that was right pretty, and applies to this proposed dam too," Farley said. "Grace, now will you sing us your own songs?"

Farley strummed his lap dulcimer while she sang a song about Jack Creek, combining words from her father's poems, her memories as a child, her own experience coming home. In a high clear voice like the sound of moving water, Grace sang of early morning mist thinning, otters splashing in the sun, kingfishers skimming riffles, trout rising to the surface at dusk, moonlight flashing on a still pool. She sang about clean water, tranquility, and community.

Everyone was quiet. As Grace started to climb down, Farley whipped out his fiddle, and the crowd sang together, "Happy Birthday to Grace." Sally Bee carried over one of Ruby's blueberry pies covered with candles ablaze for her to blow out. Grace had figured Ruby and Jared had forgotten, but they had all conspired together to surprise her.

Neighbors crowded around to compliment her voice and the simple words of her song. Grace felt no vanity, but gratitude to share their love of the creek. Jared said he never knew she could sing so well. As a birthday present, Sam handed Grace her father's fly rod that he had rigged with new line. Grace was grateful for the gift of good neighbors and the gift of her voice to call others to awareness.

21

"But when is the moment I'll know?" Grace pressed Sam for an answer as she opened the pasture gates. They were cleaning the field after the festival. "I mean, you decided you were a pacifist when you shot the rabbit with the arrow; that was your moment of realization." She wanted to know when she could make a commitment to believing anything.

"I take a long time to make decisions," Sam said. "Wear your sword as long as you can."

"In science you look for a hypothesis," she said. "In poetry I look for a metaphor. That is, we both see the similarity between different things. Bing! The lightbulb. The moment of epiphany, James Joyce calls it, when something insignificant before, now dawns on you as real."

"I collect bugs that turn into data points on a graph. They look like a random scatter, but I stare until I make a connection and draw a line. You look at all the data points as choices, and your mind runs down the consequences of each alternative."

"So, are you saying I am random scatter?" She was peeved.

"Give me those, Grace," Sam took four folding chairs, too heavy for her sore back, and loaded them into the pickup. "You're always muddying the water, stirring up sediment. You have to let the silt sift to the bottom. Wait for the water to be clear. Quakers call it 'waiting for clearness.'"

"We are building momentum to fight the dam," she said. "I'm excited people came to the festival and took rides on the river."

"Be still," Sam caught her to slow her down before he finished loading tables to drive back to the church hall.

"I want to know now if we can get scenic-river status. I want to know now—" Grace continued thinking—if she would live happily ever after. If she would have kids. Sam drove the truck to the road. She walked behind to close the gates.

Grace was in turmoil. She was as happy as she had ever been, family all around her, neighbors who agreed the river was worth saving. Yet she was still restless.

At Taizé in France, the monastery where Grace had camped at New Years with a thousand European students, the monk Emil had quoted St. Paul: "I want you to be happy. What I want for you is your happiness." Because the temperature was below freezing in January in the large canvas tents that bunked forty students, Grace had moved indoors to a "silent" house, and for two days had written in her journal. Her only acquaintance with the Bible were stories Ruby used to tell her. Later, flipping through pages of Paul's letters, she could not find the passage Emil quoted. I can be happy, she thought, if I can just decide what I want.

What more did she want than family and friends?

After a late supper the night of the festival, Sam was washing dishes and Grace was drying. At the table Ruby, Amos, and Jared were drinking coffee. Grace was pleased how comfortable Jared acted at the farm. Ruby had put him in his place and put him to work. Grace was initially nervous with Sam and Jared at the supper table, but they got along fine. Still plagued by what more she wanted, Grace asked Ruby, "What makes you happy?"

"Happy? It's not the celebrations like today or birthday parties. It's seeing a ray of sun on the dust rising when I sweep." Grace considered little things when she was milking or walking fence lines—moths on wispy wish-ball weeds. Ruby said, "To them that believe, all things that happen, happen for the good."

Sam said, "Jared, you dry the dishes so Grace can put them away." Grace did not think he had ever helped wash dishes, but he stood to help and asked Sam about his inventory of insects.

Sam said, "I'm working slowly but surely."

"Amos," Grace said, "what makes you happy?"

"Belonging here with Clara and Ruby, even though I am cantankerous."

Grace stacked casserole dishes in the pantry and walked back to the sink. "Sam, what makes you happy?"

"Getting dirty and tired, then getting clean and rested.

Blueberry pie." They had all taken turns before supper in the one shower. Sam and Amos and Jared finished off the last of Ruby's pies.

"Jared, what makes you happy?"

"A fast car, good liquor, and fast women." Amos chuckled at that.

"You are all humoring me," she laughed.

"What about yourself, Grace?" asked Ruby, sitting at the table.

She stopped to think for a minute. "Getting strong enough to lift a bale of hay by myself." Grace was scared that her satisfaction wouldn't last. "With Farley's spring water, my back will get better so I can lift bales again."

Ruby said, "And could you keep your heart in wonder at the daily miracles in your life, your pain would not seem less wondrous than your joy."

"Amen to that. It's time for me to walk home," Amos said.

"Can I drive you?" Jared offered.

"Heavens no," Amos replied. "But thanks. I would like a ride sometime in your sports car."

When Grace said good night to Amos from the porch, she said seriously, "Maybe it's good my father never saw the hemlocks on the ridge dying from acid rain, after watching the chestnuts die in his lifetime. Or the half-acre lots spreading out from Jackson."

After Amos left, Ruby went to her room and Sam went to his bus, Grace sat up late talking with Jared. He had accepted Ruby's invitation to stay over in the spare room.

"What do you want to be, Jared?" Grace asked. "After business school."

"Marry a rich wife so I can be a country banker, raise dogs and shoot ducks. And you," Jared said to irritate her, "you'll be just like Eleanor when you grow up."

"Thanks a lot," she said. "You mean neurotic and feather-headed. Maybe that's why I act so stubborn, so no man will ever treat me the way you and Tolly condescend to Eleanor. I'm not

145

sure I want children. I don't want to get married. If I tell Eleanor, she will just say, don't worry your sweet head about that. Jared, I can't join the Junior League, marry a Main Street stockbroker who wears a three-piece suit, drive a Country Squire with Irish setters and carpool kids to dancing and riding lessons."

Jared said, "So how long do you intend to live on the farm?"

"After college I can teach school in McDowell," she said, "unless they flood the creek."

He said, "But if you keep farming, you'll age faster, working outdoors in the cold. Keeping up the farm will cost more than it ever earns. What are you going to do for social life and intellectual challenge in the country?"

"Cities lack community," she said. "Life should be lived together. Here I'll live among people who care for me."

He said, "Ruby won't last forever, you know." Grace did not want to hear that. "You'll never use your good mind and education, teaching in a county high school or married to a poor man."

"Community is commitment and struggle," she said. "I have no anxiety because I'm needed here. I'll heal and grow here."

"You can't eat sunsets," he said.

"You sound like Eleanor," she said. "Did she send you as her emissary?"

"No, in fact, I benefit if you do stay here," Jared said. "Look, Dabney, I mean Grace, you should know. If you don't leave the farm, Eleanor will cut you out of her will. She says you don't need any inheritance if you marry a farm boy."

"Does she hate this place and my father so much?" she asked.

He said, "Tolly encourages her. You threaten his security."

"He uses all her money that he wants," she said.

"Not when she dies. Her money all goes to you," he said. "So he wants her to change her will. I have nothing to benefit telling you this."

Grace said nothing for a minute, "Well, I'm not going to live with Eleanor just to be rich when she dies. Does she want to punish me, because her mother punished her for marrying my father?"

"I can't answer that," Jared said matter-of-factly. "What about this guy, Sam? You two seem to like each other. But he can't support you wading rivers."

"We're just friends," Grace said.

"I do envy your land and free spirit," he said. "I can't break away from Richmond."

"Jared," she asked, "why did you have to hit me?"

"When? I don't remember."

"At the Lindbergs in June."

"I really don't remember; I must have been drunk. I'm sorry."

Grace was moved by Jared's apparent, unaccustomed sincerity. What if the power company did flood the farm? He voiced her own concerns about Sam. He could give her no assurances of security. Ruby would die someday. How can I choose? What can I contribute? Grace prayed.

Words and music move me. I speak with my voice about my home and my feelings. I can sing.

Ruby had told her, "Be still and know that I am God. Seek ye first the kingdom of heaven."

22

"I can't figure where we are." Amos turned the map upside down to get a better fix.

"Let me have a look," Farley said.

"You can't read," Amos said.

"You can't sing," Farley retorted.

Driving through a cloud, with five-foot visibility, Grace inched the farm truck over a mountain pass above the Blue Ridge Parkway. She was driving Farley Dodge to compete in the Old Time Fiddlers' Convention at Galax. Amos insisted on coming so Grace wouldn't rile the country folk by traveling alone with a half-black man.

Because of the cloud she could barely see chicory growing by the roadside. Suddenly a deer darted from the woods across the road, and she braked to miss it.

"Stay on your own side of the road in case somebody's coming the other way," Amos said.

"You can't pull off the road with no shoulder," Farley said. "What time're we supposed to get there?"

"Y'all hush. Too many drivers. Farley, your schedule says the fiddling doesn't start until seven. We'll get there in plenty of time. I don't think this small road is on the map," Grace said.

"The map says second turn right after Mabry Mill," Amos said.

They climbed into the cloud on the mountain in hairpin turns and switchbacks. Down the other side, they descended from the thinning mist through a small settlement of homesteads, log barns, split-rail fences, and gnarled apple trees. Since there were no turn-offs by the road, Grace kept driving five miles until they reached a two-lane highway.

At the first filling station, she asked, "Where's Galax?"

"This is it. You're here," the attendant said. "If you want the fiddle festival, head north and take a right at the fairground."

At the festival gate Grace stopped to ask where they could park.

"Camping inside is for contestants only," said a man in a Galax Moose hat.

"We have a contestant," Amos said.

"You have to be registered," the man said. Grace could see the gatekeeper was uneasy with the black man in the truck. Except for their childish bickering, she was glad Amos had come along with Farley.

Amos said, "Show him the paper, Farley."

The man at the gate examined the registration. "Is this you?" He nodded to Amos. Amos pointed at Farley.

"We've never had a colored contestant," the Galax Moose said.

"He's a fiddler," Grace said.

"And I'm his lawyer," Amos said.

"Well, do you have a band you want to camp with?" the man asked.

"No, it's just us," she said.

They drove down the hill by the cement grandstand. A mustard-yellow circus tent covered the stage and an area behind it. The banner over the stage read, "Galax Lodge #733 Loyal Order of Moose. 38th Annual Old Fiddlers' Convention." Banjo players were already competing.

"Amos, you're not a lawyer," Farley said. "You don't even look like one."

"Nope, and you, by jingo, don't look like the rest of us crackers," Amos replied.

In the large flat field Grace pulled the truck into an empty space between a van and a horse trailer. She set up her tent, and Amos stretched a tarp over a grassy area for sitting and cooking, and over the bed of the truck for Farley and him to sleep. Amos was shuffling his feet to the mountain music. Tuning and blending together, all around them, were southern voices, basses thumping, and high whining fiddles.

"Ruby packed enough food for a week," Grace said, opening the picnic box. "Let's eat chicken."

"Let's eat Ruby's cake first," said Farley. "Amos, stop jiving and read the rules for me." Farley handed Amos the program.

"It says you have to play an authentic folk tune. You can enter only one contest outside of band. Says bands must have a banjo, a fiddle, and a guitar to qualify. Says you fiddle for one minute. Sixty seconds."

"That's all?" Grace chirped.

Amos said, "The program shows a hundred and thirty-four fiddlers. Tonight they pick twelve to play longer for the semi-finals tomorrow. Farley, you're listed right here, number one-twenty," and he pointed the name to Farley.

On folding chairs in the campsite next door, two men played banjo in claw-hammer style. The younger one in khaki pants and a blue Oxford shirt was copying the old farmer's drop-thumb fingering.

"Do y'all want coffee now, Amos? Farley?" she asked. They shook their heads. She had borrowed a Coleman stove from Harry Benton.

"I want to walk around and listen," Farley said. He picked up his fiddle case.

"We better come with you," Amos said.

As Amos, Grace, and Farley walked the rows of tents and pickups, musicians leaned their heads together, picking and grinning. One bluegrass cluster in matching red shirts played fiddle, guitar, mandolin, and bass. The small mandolin player sang tenor, and the tall guitarist sang bass in harmony, "Ruby, Ruby, why are you mad at your man?" After they repeated the tune a few times, each separate instrument alternated, alone, louder and fancier.

Down the way a wizened old man in overalls slapped his hand on a bass as tall as he was. He looked up and flashed a toothless smile. Next to him, a man who needed a shave stuck his lit cigarette under his strings of his metal-faced guitar, string-side facing up. He slid the neck of a bottle to make the strings warble

Hawaiian.

"That's a Dobro," Farley said.

Musicians wore clean farm clothes—overalls, jeans, plaid shirts, and work shoes. One man wore a T-shirt that said, "Support Our Boys in Vietnam." Another T-shirt said, "POW-MIA." Among the crowd were college kids dressed in sports clothes, but Grace recognized no one her age. In her jeans and straw hat, she blended with the farm folk.

Bits of gospel songs floated by—"I'll Fly Away" and "Farther Along." Grace overheard, "That's always been a favorite of mine." And "Do you know 'I'll Be All Smiles Tonight' or 'Pretty Polly'"? A mandolin player said to a fiddler, "Play a stretch, and I'll pick it up."

The loudspeaker announced, "Fiddlers, come to the gold tent."

As Amos, Grace, and Farley approached the stage, they passed a row of concessions selling barbecue, roasted corn, beer, and lemonade. On tables were records, straw hats, leather belts, and old fiddles for sale.

"I'd love some cotton candy," Farley said.

"Won't your hands get sticky?" Grace asked. "Why don't you wait? Farley, what're you going to play?"

"I'll see what others play ahead of me."

Farley joined the line of fiddlers going into the back of the yellow tent. Farley wore a white starched shirt that made his dark skin shine. Grace had not seen a black face in the entire crowd. None of the contestants tuning and joking among themselves turned to speak to Farley. No one had been rude, but Farley passed among them as invisible.

"Good luck, Farley, we'll be sitting in the middle of the bleachers," she said.

The concrete grandstand had a high metal roof. Amos and Grace walked up six rows and sat on the hard concrete. Farm ladies in the stand had brought foam cushions to sit on, while their husbands wandered among the pick-up bands in the campground. Lawn chairs covered the grass between grandstand and the stage.

152

On plywood boards to the right of the stage, dancers stepped to the music. An identical father and teenage son in bib jeans with striped elastic suspenders clogged in unison, moving no muscle above their knees. Their deadpan faces clearly showed the same high-cheek bone structure. Next to the men, a big-breasted woman packed into her jeans and tank top hopped with no rhythmic relevance to the music. On the path in front of the grandstand, Grace watched two high school girls, slouched over in halter tops, walk by sideways like crabs. An older couple had matching cowboy boots, cowboy hats, and kelly-green western shirts with pearl buttons. The man was so fat that his overhanging belly buried his belt.

In the first fifty or so entries, eight played renditions of "Orange Blossom Special." Others repeated "Turkey in the Straw," "Arkansas Traveler," and "Old Joe Clark." Farley said he'd play something nobody else played. The announcer kept the fiddlers moving across the stage fast, alternating between microphones on the right and left. Grace was surprised how bad some of the playing was. One fellow kept sawing the same intro-phrase over and over for a minute. One pint-size boy played "Twinkle, twinkle, little star" to tremendous applause. A fellow had a fiddle painted like the Confederate flag, with the white cross diagonal across the red and blue. Contestants came from cities like Richmond or Asheville, from Cambridge, Massachusetts, and somebody all the way from Dublin, Ireland.

The emcee introduced a twelve-year-old girl who started playing a flashy Beethoven violin concerto. "Never knew a fiddle could sound like that," the woman next to Grace said. Halfway, the little girl switched to "Orange Blossom Special." The audience hooted and stomped at the familiar tune. They clapped the most for very old men and the little girl in crinolines. The next fiddler had so much hair on his face, all Grace could see was beard and felt hat. He leaned his fiddle against his waist instead of his chin like the others.

The sun setting behind the grandstand cast pink light on the blue layers of the Blue Ridge behind the stage. Grace was getting a sore behind from sitting on concrete.

Finally, the guy with the microphone announced, "Number one-twenty, Farley Dodge from Jackson, Virginia."

When Farley stepped into the lights, some man in the grandstand yelled, "What's a darky doing at Galax?"

"Shut up and listen," Amos stood up and said. "Give the man a chance." Under his breath, Amos muttered, "Anyway, he's more than half Indian." Grace was proud of Amos.

Farley slowly started an Irish jig that changed to an Appalachian reel. He let loose, fingers flying, his bow burning the strings, bagpipe drone and playful tune at the same time, faster than the cloggers by the stage could dance, poignant, mournful, and joyous. There was modest clapping.

"Hard to keep my feet still. He did good," Amos said, "if only them judges was listening to him, instead of looking."

Grace handed Farley a paper cone of pink cotton candy when he came out of the gold tent.

As she fell asleep in her tent an hour later, she could pick out single strands from the mountain of melodies. "There is a Balm in Gilead to heal the sin-sick soul." "My Home's across the Blue Ridge Mountains." "Will the Circle be Unbroken?" Tunes rang in her sleep all night just the way she heard the river at the farm. She felt comfort in the dark that no one let the threads of music drop until the day broke light.

Grace woke to drizzling rain Saturday. Amos and Farley slept dry under the tarp in the back of the truck. Passing the men's shower house, she tore down a hand-lettered paper sign, "Whites Only." She never did see Farley use the public facility.

Grace stood in line for the portable toilets behind an old farm lady in a gingham dress, who held an umbrella. Somebody ahead wore a clear plastic dry-cleaner bag with holes for her head and arms.

"It always rains at Galax," the lady said. "I don't know what is worst, mud or dust." She wore black lace-up shoes like Charlotte

154

Dabney used to wear. "I been coming since my husband competed in 1957. He's dead now ten years."

The woman said, "This year, there's too many Yankees and hippies. Used to be it was all musicians came here. I'm not going to camp tonight. Makes me scared with them college kids drinking and tie-dyed hippies doing drugs."

Too bad the lady wanted to leave Galax because of people drinking too much, Grace thought. She had seen no one using drugs, but probably couldn't tell if she had.

"Young people just ain't raised right anymore," the lady said. "My two sons died in Vietnam, you know. I'm from over to Mouth of Wilson. Where're you from, dear?"

"McDowell County."

"My sister married a Cline from Jackson, but she died in '68." It sounded like the old lady's whole family had died. She talked so much she was probably lonely living by herself.

"I'm sorry you're leaving," Grace said.

When she came back to the truck, a man was asking Farley to play with his band. "Our fiddler didn't show up," he said, "and we need a fiddle to compete."

"Well, sure, I'd be honored," Farley said.

Amos said to Grace, "They heard last night that Farley is the best fiddler here, and they want to win."

"Come over to practice with us?" the man asked.

"I can play anything I hear," Farley said.

Saturday night after the fiddling finals and the old-timey band contest, the man on stage announced the winners. "Lloyd Pillow, first fiddler. Grover Bottom, second. And Farley Dodge, third." The band Farley played with, the Grayson Highland Ramblers, was fourth, out of the money.

"Farley, congratulations," Amos said. "But I can't believe you didn't win."

"I didn't play to win," Farley said. "I play for the sake of the music. The fiddle plays. The music plays itself through me."

"I can't believe it," Grace said again. "You played better'n

155

anybody else."

"If I'd played to win," Farley said, "I would have been nervous. I might 'a' been on that record album, and if I was to get famous, then people would come find my spring and bother me. I think about the music rather than the winning."

23

In the kitchen of the farmhouse, Ruby braided Grace's hair in careful plaits, tight against her head. "Your hair's not quite long enough yet, but it's growing. Your hair is darker now," Ruby said. "When you were ten, it was gold as wheat and long as your waist."

"I remember," Grace said, "you used to check my scalp for ticks after I played in the woods. And braid my hair so tight before school that my forehead pulled upwards and my eyeballs pulled apart."

Grace remembered once when one of her pigtails came undone in Richmond at the Country Club pool. Eleanor had dropped her off alone, just after her father's death. She had cried because she couldn't braid her own hair as Ruby had always done. Finally, the maid in the locker room braided her long hair, too loose.

At eighteen, Grace still wanted mother-figures to comfort her when she hurt. Ruby never got married, never had her own children, but cared for everyone in the valley. Ruby had really been Grace's mother more than Eleanor, who set conditions on loving her daughter, like grades and clothes.

Mother, Grace wanted to say, do you hold a grudge against me that I was born before you finished college? On Wednesday, she spoke over the phone, "Eleanor, I want a chance to talk to you this weekend."

"Oh, I'll see you at all the parties," Eleanor said. "Do you have your clothes ready yet? You'll need an outfit for the luncheon and dinner, and Christi's ball. If you need a new dress, I'll be glad to pay for it."

Grace knew they would have no chance to talk seriously at the parties.

Mid August, she drove to Richmond for the debutante party of a neighbor, who had graduated from St. Catherine's a year ahead of her. Christi had just finished a year at Sweet Briar. Her father

157

was Grace's dentist, and their parents played bridge together.

Past noon Friday, Grace walked into her mother's empty house. Not even Ophelia was home. In her closet, she pushed through the hangers of bright pastel dresses and pulled on a royal-blue linen sheath. She found some matching blue Pappagallo flats and hoped the elastic dent around her ankles from her socks would go away.

At lunch Christi told Grace, "I knew I would marry Kip for sure this spring. I turned around in the train station and lost sight of him for a moment in the crowd. I knew then I couldn't live without him." Christi whispered secretly to Grace. "We want to get married right away, but Mother insisted that I come out into society first. We'll wait until Christmas so Daddy can pay these bills, before he goes into more debt for a wedding reception. You'll be a bridesmaid, won't you?"

After the luncheon, Grace went to look at evening dresses at Montaldo's. She walked past jewelry, scarves, shoes, and sports clothes. She passed scrawny manikins with jutting pelvic bones, modeling the winter suits. A Richmond neighbor, five years older than Grace, modeled for Lord and Taylor's ads in *The New Yorker*. In Richmond on holidays, she was so skinny, Grace could barely see her sideways. Grace had always felt too fat, but didn't care anymore. Tough, she thought, Sam says I'm athletic.

The fall fashion colors were mustard orange called pumpkin and deep plum called aubergine. Grace liked purple, but she hated when colors she liked were fashionable. Since she still wore the blue linen dress, the salesladies smiled at her. Imagine if I had worn jeans or milking overalls, she thought.

"Wear clothes that make you look rich," Eleanor had said to her. "Make other people think you are better than they are." Jared was a good example of that strategy.

Grace walked by the make-up counter. Eager briefly to be a teenager, when she was thirteen, she had worn lipstick for half a year. She never did have time for nail polish. On the elevator an elderly man in a brown uniform pushed the lever up and down. All day he rode one floor up and one floor down.

"Grace, glad to see you home," Mrs. Curran greeted her in the second-floor bridal department. For cheap long dresses to wear at debutante balls, Grace bought sample bridesmaids' dresses off the sale rack. She fit the standard size eight.

"Nice to see you, Mrs. Curran," Grace smiled. She liked the trim short lady with the black bun of hair.

Mrs. Curran pulled out a pink dress with puffy sleeves, and Grace shook her head. Too hot for dancing in August, and too prissy. After wearing work boots all summer, she didn't know if any of her heels would fit or if she could walk in them. At Cotillion, when she was fourteen, she had worn her first high heels in a cha-cha demonstration at the Holly Ball. Between sixth and ninth grades, she and Christi carpooled to Cotillion. Christi had met Kip in ninth grade and had dated him since then.

"Pretty soon we'll be preparing your wedding too," Mrs. Curran said.

"I'm barely eighteen." Grace knew the lady was only being polite, but why was there this emphasis on getting married? Was the whole goal of education to marry a rich boy? The measurement of success at Sweet Briar was the size of engagement rings and newspaper announcements. She wasn't ready yet to settle down for the rest of her life.

Grace thanked Mrs. Curran and checked another sale rack. She needed a ball dress. From Eleanor, she did inherit the consolation in buying new clothes. Fingering the fabric of the dresses on any rack, Grace could pick the most expensive dress, but refused to spend the money, as whatever she wore at the farm would get dirty. On the half-price rack, she found a white silk pants suit.

Eleanor had said to buy a dress. Grace tried on an Indian-silk long dress, pink-and-red paisley print with long sleeves; size four, but it fit perfectly. The more expensive the designer, the smaller the size. Then she found a floor-length brown crepe-silk culotte dress with two wide stripes of electric-pink and chartreuse below her knees; a tiny button at each shoulder held up the heavy draping crepe. The skirt was so full that she could lift the hem waist-high as she twirled with her arms outstretched. Grace bought all three outfits.

At the house, when Grace returned at five, Eleanor was on her way out the door. Tolly was waiting in the car. "We're stopping first for cocktails," she said. "You can walk to the Burtons for dinner, and your escort will drive you from there. Why, Grace, you must get your hair styled."

"Why do you always want me to cut my hair? I'm letting it grow. Eleanor, by the way, what ever happened to my pigtails? Did we save them?"

"To your what, dear?"

"My braids that you cut off when I was ten."

"I have no idea. Why I think I threw them away. Grace, I'll be late."

"Wait a minute. I remember when you cut my hair. Actually you botched it, and I had to go to the beauty parlor."

"Really, dear, that was years ago. Braids were old-fashioned." Eleanor wanted to leave. "You were going to summer camp, I recall. Short hair dries faster when you swim." She walked away to the car where Tolly was waiting.

Grace muttered to herself, "You just couldn't spend the time braiding my hair the way Ruby did." When Grace had entered fifth grade in Richmond, with a class full of strangers, she didn't recognize herself. In June, Eleanor had cut her braids, and in September, Grace got glasses and, later that fall, braces on her teeth. When she first put on the glasses, she could actually see leaves in the trees and read road signs.

That year, when she was ten, Grace read *Jane Eyre*. The next year, in sixth grade, the eye doctor told her not to read so much. She was smarter than the other girls, but she was behind socially. She was the only one who raised her hand in Health class when the teacher asked who did not know what Kotex was. She never forgot how embarrassed she felt.

Gee, Grace thought in objective amazement, still in the driveway watching Eleanor and Tolly drive away, I'm still behind. I'm the only virgin my age I know now.

At the dinner, Grace was overwhelmed by a hundred people milling around on the Burtons' lawn, drinking cocktails. She wore the new red-and-pink silk dress. Jared's classmate Punch walked over to her. "It's grand to see you, Grace." He laughed and poured champagne down her back, perfectly good willed and drunk. Punch meant the soaking somehow as a friendly gesture. Punch's sister Edith apologized, "I'll pay for the cleaning bill." Grace nodded gamely. She would not send a bill.

With a wet back, she found her name on a table between Brad, a good tennis player she had dated once, and Kenneth, her embarrassing ninth-grade crush. Since their mothers had driven them to parties in seventh and eighth grades, Kenneth had grown a foot taller and put on contact lenses. Christi was obviously trying to be nice.

"Have you heard?" Kenneth asked Brad. "The state just closed a company in Hopewell for dumping rat poison called Kepone into the James River for the last thirty years. The poison will be in river sediments for the next century, and the governor may close fishing in the James River."

Grace couldn't help but notice that anyone can become an environmentalist when pollution happens in his own backyard.

After dinner, Grace asked Kenneth to stop at her house for a minute. She ran upstairs and changed into the one-of-a-kind brown dress with pink and yellow-green stripes at the hem.

For Christi's debutante party, six hundred people filled the Oriental-carpeted entrance hall and the brocade-wallpaper ballroom at the Country Club. Grace carried fruit punch to Christi in the receiving line under the towering oak trees on the marble patio overlooking the putting green and swimming pools. Kip was in a chair. He was hardly able to stand. As a joke, the night before, some fraternity brothers had fed him liquor, then left him passed out in the sauna in the men's locker room for an hour. He could have died, Grace thought; protect me from stupid people.

From nine to midnight, the orchestra played watered-down rock 'n' roll and foxtrot, for which Cotillion was supposed to prepare Grace. On the polished dance floor were girls in swirling pink skirts, in the arms of men in black tuxedos; everyone seemed to be getting drunk on the free, flowing liquor. Kenneth, her designated escort, had disappeared; dorky guys asked her to dance, probably prompted by Christi's mother. "Maybe you'll meet somebody" was Eleanor's maxim for debutante parties and weddings. Maybe, because these Richmond guys did not interest Grace anymore, she had a great time waltzing with old men she knew from playing tennis.

Other girls wore puffy pastel dresses; in the brown dress she felt wicked like Bette Davis as Jezebel. She considered stepping into a shadow on the golf course, loosing one button that held up the heavy fabric, letting it drop, and slipping into the pond. She might have, as a mysterious-woman gesture, but the muddy pond was too shallow to hide her.

The photographer snapped Grace with Eleanor and Tolly in front of red velvet curtains. She had no chance to talk privately with Eleanor.

Christi whispered to Grace, "I'll throw you my bouquet at Christmas."

"No thanks, Christi, not yet," she said.

Grace arrived home just after Eleanor and Tolly. "Mother, I want to talk," she said, in the hallway.

"Tomorrow." Eleanor kicked off her heels.

"No, tomorrow I am leaving early," Grace said.

"All right. Tolly, bring me a nightcap," Eleanor called to him in the hall. "We had a grand party. I didn't know you had dated one of Kip's fraternity brothers." Tolly handed Eleanor the drink and then went upstairs.

"I left him because he drank too much." That was also true.

"Oh," Eleanor swallowed. She couldn't refute that. "I see." Grace thought her mother was such a hypocrite.

"Don't you understand there is more to life," Grace said, "to my life at least, than drinking at the Country Club? I don't want to be judged by what I look like and can pay for."

"You judge me. Your goody-goody sobriety is an affront to me."

"You taught me high standards. What you expect of me is not who I am."

"You're being narrow minded," Eleanor said.

"By not wanting to be like you?" Grace said. "I'm not condemning you, Eleanor. I just can't be a polite Junior League wife with three kids. I want to go to graduate school."

"The more educated you are," Eleanor said, "the fewer men there will be. If you have a PhD, you can't marry a gasoline mechanic."

"I can if I love him, but I don't want to get married and have kids."

"You haven't even started college yet," Eleanor said. "You don't have to worry your sweet head about that." Grace knew she would say that.

"Mother, why do you begrudge me so much? What did I ever do?"

"I lost ten years of my life in the mountains," Eleanor said. "I don't want you to bury yourself there too."

"I don't consider the farm being buried. Don't you see I can get to know my father?"

"Nonsense."

"Are you angry that you had to marry my father?" Grace asked. "Surely you must have loved him at some point."

"Tom was not the class that my parents had raised me to expect. I asked my mother for money for an abortion, and she refused. 'It's your own fault,' she said. 'So live with it.' You're so much like Tom, you know," Eleanor said.

"But you chose to leave when I was a child." By drinking, Eleanor neglected her, even when she lived there. "Mother, when did you start drinking?"

163

"Your grandfather, my father, was a drunk," Eleanor said. "My mother Charlotte ran his company, without, of course, letting her work show in public. She'd balance the books at a secretary's desk, outside her husband's walnut-paneled office. My father had the leather chair and ceremonial desk."

Grace was silent; she'd never heard this story. Eleanor said, "I learned to drink from my father. But that's neither here nor there." Eleanor couldn't sound sincere for long. "Look," Eleanor said, standing up. "You can stay up all night. I'm going upstairs."

Grace stopped in the kitchen, but there was no milk or juice in the refrigerator. She found none of Ophelia's cookies. Like her house, Eleanor was empty. Grace feared she would suffer the same spiritual hollowness she observed in her mother. Eleanor valued her daughter's achievements because she had so little of her own esteem. Eleanor was childish and dependent. Grace could expect no comfort from her; instead, Grace would always have to give. Instead of hating or resenting Eleanor, she began to pity her.

Used to early rising, at the farm Grace never stayed up past ten. At one, wired after dancing, she scanned the bookshelf by her bedside. Eleanor's house had no other books. Whenever Grace slept in someone's house, she would raid the bookshelves and read late into the night. Off the shelf of her own childhood books, she pulled a copy of Laura Ingalls Wilder's *These Happy Golden Years* and read half an hour.

Grace felt sucked dry and yearned for someone to rock and shelter her. I don't have the reservoir of being loved that other children grow up with, Grace thought as she lay in bed.

Then she remembered Ruby who had mothered her until she was ten. And now, again. There was her father, before, and Amos and Sam now. Grace fell asleep thinking of her family at the farm.

24

Go to the top of the mountain to find peace, Ruby had said at the square dance. To tap her feelings, Grace was looking for memories of her childhood. She decided to climb the hill as far as the spring that served as water source for the farm. The French word for spring is *la source*, she thought. She had returned to McDowell County to find her source.

When Eleanor hassled her to move back to Richmond, Grace replied, "I'll keep the farm long enough to remember where I come from."

At the top of the orchard, Grace saw bushes of orange butterfly weed in the unmown fencerow. She was learning plant names from Amos: bloodroot and liverwort, birch and beech, dogwood and ironwood, jewelweed and butterfly weed. Attracted to the same shade, orange monarch butterflies were landing on the inflorescence of butterfly weed.

Oh, if only attraction were so easy, thought Grace. I don't mean black and white races. Sam was as similar to her as any other person she had met, but decided that he seemed more of a brother than a boyfriend. She was unwilling to lose Sam as a friend if they ever broke up as sweethearts.

Grace remembered when Amos had first taken her walking in April. She remembered eight years earlier following her father up the hill and playing in the grass while he pruned these apple trees that she would prune again after the first frost. In the woods above the orchard now, she passed twenty-foot-tall striped maple and hickory, new-growth trees where the woods had been logged when she was born.

Self-reliant and stubborn as any hill man, her father had been insulted when Eleanor's father offered him money at their wedding, so he sold an acre of old-growth timber, dear to him, to support a wife and new baby.

The ferns hanging over the path whipped her knees wet with

165

dew. Grace walked the path uphill—parallel to the stream that divided the house and the fields, the path bending away and returning to the stream. When rocks rose on the right side, she forded, balancing across a ledge without getting her feet wet. Her leather boots were heavy and hot on the August day.

Farms used springs on the mountain for water supply. The black PVC pipe carrying spring water to the house followed the streambed, too. The second dam would be right above their farm. In the valley the power company would collect water behind the first dam to pump up from the lower reservoir to the upper reservoir at the top of the mountain. Water pumped uphill would follow the same course downhill, underground through 30-foot-diameter tunnels. They would dig miles of tunnels inside the mountain, with reversible turbines to pump water uphill or for falling water to turn for power. The steep slope on Bluff Mountain, which caught her breath, was what attracted the power company in the first place.

A heavy whomp-whomp—like a tiny helicopter on the TV news in Vietnam—erupted suddenly at her feet. Grace froze. A brown ball of feathers, smaller than a football, flew from the underbrush, in order to lead a predator from her nest. Over her shoulder Grace saw six speckled-brown tennis-balls scurrying away to hide. Just twelve feet ahead of her on the trail, the mother ruffed grouse chirped staccato in alarm to lead Grace away. Her feathers were crosshatched gray and brown like herringbone tweed.

"Okay, I see you feign a broken wing," she spoke. "I'm not going to hurt your chicks."

August was late to give birth, so the mother's first clutch must not have survived. Maybe that's why she was especially nervous and protective. As Grace followed, the bird limped dragging a wing—twenty, then thirty feet ahead—staying on the path, then disappearing when Grace was well enough away from her nest.

At her feet Grace bent down to examine Indian pipes, all-white blossoms and stalks, a plant that grows without

166

photosynthesis. Instead, it takes nutrients, as a mushroom does, from decaying leaves, deep mulch rotting into humus, rich with earthworms and burrowing bugs. Under a layer of leaves Grace grabbed a handful of soft brown duff. If the power company cut down the forest to build the dam, this rich hillside would erode. Soil in the pasture was thin, too rocky for tillage, adequate only for pasturing limited animals. That's why the creek folk had handicrafts to sell.

McDowell County was certainly scenic, but not as fertile as it was before their great-grandfathers cut off the trees. Really, though, mountain land never was as fertile as the Shenandoah Valley or Tidewater. Just remote. That's why her ancestors had settled there. No one to meddle until the power company came along to flood the valley.

When the black drinking-water pipe veered to the right, away from the main stream, Grace crossed again and followed it for twenty yards to a spring. Winded and hot from walking the steep grade in August heat, she sat on the moss bank. At two-thousand-feet elevation, the farm was naturally ten degrees cooler than Tidewater. In the city, asphalt roads and concrete buildings stored even more heat. If it was eighty-five degrees in McDowell that day, it must have been over a hundred in Richmond. Grace was grateful to cup her hands for a drink from the spring. The water was clean; nothing else was uphill except the Forest Service boundary and beyond that, West Virginia.

Grace scooped out leaves that had fallen into the pool so that the drinking-water intake would not clog. Amos cleaned all the neighbors' spring pools regularly when he ranged in the hills. From the bottom she gathered twigs and leaves, preserved by the cold water, and tiny hemlock rosettes from the surface. Close up she could see bubbles escaping from the sand. Spirally up, slowly released, the bubbles swirled into a different element than underground.

Hemlocks overhead shaded the spring and scented the grove when the scant wind moved their boughs. Set in a fold of the hill, the hemlocks too were shaded. Grace liked to think that hemlocks themselves breathed out cold air, rather than the fact that they grew here only on a cold north-facing slope.

Beyond the spring she recognized the red plump fruit of ginseng, the old-age tonic Amos had showed her in the spring. "Sang," ginseng's mountain nickname, was an aphrodisiac—actual or superstition. Any love potion works if you believe in it. Being eighteen was an aphrodisiac too.

Refreshed by hemlock shade, Grace decided to walk farther. She had never been to the top of the hill west of the farm, where the hermit had met God. She returned to the stream to find the headwaters.

"Sang" was the French word for blood, *le sang*, she reflected as she walked. Blood for kinship. Family roots anchored her to McDowell just like ginseng roots. "Sang and singing made," Grace remembered a poem by Wallace Stevens about a woman walking by the sea: "There never was a world for her except the one she sang, and singing, made." Living in McDowell was her groundtruthing.

As she climbed, the sound of mountain water accompanied her, background for birdcalls, boughs scraping, twigs snapping, and leaves rustling underfoot. Amos had shown her how to tread like an Indian, stepping on her heel first, then lowering the ball of her foot. The slope was getting steeper. Grace had learned as well how to save energy walking uphill by taking her weight on each alternate bended knee and then straightening the knee to pull her body one more stride-length.

Ahead the water noise increased, as water tumbled over rocks, drowning other thought. When she reached the top of the small waterfall, she saw a pool formed by the rock dam, deep enough to immerse her body, still water in contrast to the tumult below. So clear she could see the colors of gravel—pink and gray and moss-green—on the bottom. And it was cool as she knelt to wave her hand in the water.

Grace sat at the edge, slipped off her boots and socks, and

dipped her hot feet. She was tired, not just from the morning climb. She felt emotionally and physically pulled apart by Eleanor and Jared, Ruby and Sam, not by their demands but her own desire to please everyone.

When Grace was milking cows and pitchforking hay, in her daydream she screened a scenario of sipping *citron pressé* or *chocolat* at a cafe in the Alps with Will. Would she always hold out a distant fantasy of a better hero than the one she was with? Didn't she appreciate that Sam was a mud-and-blood man in the flesh?

To remind herself she doubted his judgment, her back muscles, bruised when she fell at Dolly Sods, ached from her exertion uphill. As much as his spontaneity tickled her, Sam could also endanger her by his impetuosity. His live-for-the-moment personality also meant he procrastinated deadlines and responsibilities.

How much violence did Sam repress beneath his mild-mannered pacifism? Why were men motivated to be macho, as when Jared punched her jaw in a political squabble? She didn't want to bear grudges. She would have to stand up to express her anger.

Grace guessed she must pass through developmental stages in emotional maturity just like learning to walk. Before she became a woman, it was okay, now, for her to play like a child for a while longer.

Let go, the pool seduced, drawing Grace back to the moment. She was tempted to get wet. But she had brought no bathing suit. *Take off your clothes*, half of her prompted. *Swim naked?* Inhibition restrained her. *Who would see?* No one was watching. She glanced around: rhododendron, laurel, and ferns surrounded the pool's natural privacy.

Grace stood to shuck off her jeans and pulled her T-shirt over her head. Her arms were sunburned like a field worker; otherwise, her skin was as pale as her white underwear. This summer, she had not been sunbathing at the pool or the beach, as she usually did. She was glad, though, that she was growing

169

muscles like Ruby's. What made her feel most exposed was when she took off her eyeglasses. Since she could not see the rocks well, she crouched on bent knees, sitting on the back of her ankles. From the edge, she slid under water to cover her nakedness.

The water was startling cold. Goose bumps rippled her flesh. Grace pulled out the rubber band at the base of her neck that restrained curls and dipped her head, so her hair strung out behind her on the water. In the center of the pool, four feet from every side, she could not touch bottom, so she tread water.

She submerged, rising only to breathe and slipping under again. She could feel the rumble of water flowing in and out of the pool, yet at the center, the pool was still, unruffled. She floated on her back, stretching out her arms, expanding her lungs to be buoyant. She did not struggle to stay afloat. Like the "Eureka" moment of Archimedes, she displaced as much water as her mass, yet her presence did nothing to change the pool. She would leave no trace.

Grace heard a twig break and curled her body into a ball to hide, then unfurled; most likely, a chipmunk or squirrel was dropping acorns to hoard for winter. She dog-paddled upstream where frothy water was flowing between two boulders. She pulled herself up from the deep water to the shallows and settled in a natural seat in the rocks, so that the rush of water massaged her sore back.

Although she could not focus, without her glasses, on the overlapping leaves overhead, she felt focused inside and could sense rather than see. The sheer exultation of the slight wind, sweeping leaves, and swaying boughs moved her. Grace slipped back into the pool depth.

As she floated, the world was turning like the vortex Ishmael saw from the masthead in *Moby-Dick*. When she closed her eyes, she felt she was twirling, swirling round waltzing, counter-clockwise, in the pool.

The circle was complete. Rain falls from clouds, flows downstream crashing over waterfalls, through slow silty reservoirs, from Virginia's Ridge and Valley province west of the Shenandoah Valley and from the Blue Ridge, past Piedmont towns into Tidewater estuaries, out the Chesapeake Bay to the sea, where rain returns to the sky.

I am at the center of this circle, Grace thought. At the headwaters, water spills out of the still pool; ocean surf breaks back in on the land. The green leaves of a chestnut tree fill the sky above me, as I float in a pool, on this land where ginseng roots reach deep. Like an island in a lake—Innisfree in the poem by Yeats, she felt her soul at the center of the pool was at the center of the world. Please let this mystic feeling last, she prayed. May I carry this timeless contentment with me wherever I go.

Time slowed, but kept moving. Grace shivered, scrambled over rocks at the edge, bending to keep her center of gravity low. On solid ground she straightened and shook like a dog to dry. Her hair felt cleaner than it ever did with shampoo in the shower. Her skin felt smooth as she lay on a rock warmed by the sun, before she pulled on her T-shirt and jeans.

When she put on her glasses, she saw the tooth-edge leaves of a young chestnut tree overhead. Grace could be happy, rather than always struggling to please others. A red-tailed hawk circled above like a blessing.

I must open my heart to let myself be loved, she prayed.

Uphill, near the headwaters, was enough flow to fill the pool when the rock dam stored it. Perhaps there would be enough water without exhausting the source, if you were patient, to fill a power-company reservoir at the mountaintop. Especially when supplemented by river water accumulated for a year, then pumped uphill.

Could her world accommodate the dam? Grace was a natural appeaser. Born to reconcile the contradictory worlds of her mother and father—city and country, lowground and highlands, country club and cowbarn. Opposites attract, like Eleanor and Tom. Grace knew she was struggling to make peace with her own contradictory nature.

171

Am I more like my mother than I'll admit? she considered.

She would not fight the water, angry, as her father was when he drowned. "Go with the flow," the Tao said, translated loosely. At the hearing to declare Jack Creek a scenic river, she would speak the truth as she saw it. Grace felt she was being swept into eloquence. She would listen to her voice inside and speak at the hearing about her land, her legacy.

25

On a rainy Tuesday morning before dawn at the end of August, before Grace went to college, dark sedans and rusty pickup trucks parked behind the high school. The rain had been pouring steadily for three days. Dressed in city-going clothes under their raincoats and galoshes were older couples and young families. Sally Bee carried sleeping Timmy and coaxed Loretta, stumbling half-asleep. Most country folk were accustomed to rising early, but they had left their chores half-tended that morning. Quite a few farmers in the county were doubling milking duty, that morning and night, so others could ride the bus to the state capital in Richmond.

Ladies carried hampers with chicken for dinner, thermoses of sweet tea, and sandwiches for supper. They faced a long day—three hours to the state capitol building, three hours for the hearing and sightseeing, then the ride back that night. They arranged parcels in racks overhead and settled in bus seats, eager and apprehensive. The children had never been as far as Richmond; some of the old folks had never been there, either. At the river festival—the cakewalk, craft sale, and game booths had raised the money to charter a bus so forty-six citizens in McDowell County could ask their legislators to protect Jack Creek.

"It's time to go," Ruby pressed Grace. "We have to leave without Sam."

"I'm fed up," she replied. "Just once, when it counts, can't Sam get here on time? When it really means something."

"Let's get rolling, Miss Grace," said the bus driver, starting the motor. In the front seat of the bus, on the side opposite from the driver, Ruby and Grace had an unobstructed view of the road.

"Wait one more minute, please," she said, as she walked back on the bus to find Amos. She was worried about Sam; he had promised to be there, so she wouldn't be afraid to speak at the hearing.

"Amos, you'll get angry at the hearing anyway, so—will you go look for Sam, please?" Grace gave Amos her keys.

"You know I don't drive," he said lamely.

"Sure you can. You drove Ruby to the Bentons' when she broke her leg. Try all the streams in the western edge of the county and then over the ridge in West Virginia, where he's been looking for his endangered fish."

As Amos left the bus, pressure gushed from the bus brakes. He waved as they pulled away, and the big vehicle eased down the main street of Jackson by the courthouse square, the inn, the insurance office, the general store, and the craft co-op.

"Sam keeps his own time, you know," Ruby said.

"He marches to a different drummer, all right. He was supposed to show up last night. He runs all over wading rivers by himself, and he could be hurt and stranded somewhere. I wish he would leave a message."

"You're cranky because you didn't sleep," Ruby suggested. "And you're stubborn, too."

"And you're not?" Grace was a bit abrupt, then laughed with Ruby. "I inherit it from you."

As the bus crested Shenandoah Mountain, rainclouds cleared so they could see the sun rise over the Shenandoah Valley, just as in April when Grace came west to the auction. They crossed the Valley, climbed the Blue Ridge, then coasted downhill across the Piedmont to Richmond at the head of navigation of the James River. Waters from Jack Creek flowed much the same path.

As they passed Charlottesville on Interstate 64, Grace kept an eye out along the roadside. "I wouldn't be surprised to see Sam along here flagging down the bus," she mumbled to Ruby.

As the light improved, Ruby pulled out her polyester patches to piece into quilt patterns. When Grace walked the aisle, she saw few idle hands. Millie Dorset was knitting next to Charlie, who was sleeping. Emily Puffenbarger was crocheting, Esther Conway mending socks. Grace leaned against the side of a seat to brace herself as the bus rocked. Loretta ran up and down the aisle until she settled for a nap in the seat by Ruby.

"It's important that they see us all there and hear what we have to say. Talk to these men as if they were schoolchildren," Grace said to Hilda Huffman, who was nervous about speaking in public. "Talk as if writing a letter to your granddaughter."

The bus stopped at the Capitol Square designed by Thomas Jefferson. Helen Brown, the schoolteacher, reminded them he had copied a marble temple in France. They stretched their legs for five minutes along brick walkways where tame squirrels begged peanuts. The hearing room in the Capitol was like Perry Mason's courtroom or a fine church. Polished wood rails separated the legislative committee from the pews where the McDowell people crowded. Also filling the rows were power-company employees and paid lobbyists in three-piece suits. Grace nodded to Winston Wood, the CUPCO vice-president. She was annoyed to see her stepfather sitting next to him; she needed to act calmly with Tolly as an opponent.

Grace was glad to see Gladys Conner, Dennis Schaeffer, and Emma Coleman, members of the state conservation committee to oppose the McDowell County dam, and Todd Rawlings, the director of the national river coalition. Grace handed Gladys a list of people from McDowell who wanted to speak.

"Where's Sam?" Dennis asked. "Can he report on his search for an endangered species?" Grace shrugged her shoulders, as a state senator, chairman of the scenic-river committee, called the hearing to order. She went back to sit with Ruby and Sally Bee.

Winston Wood bowed to the committee members and gestured to a scale model of the dams that his assistants carried to the front. "The McDowell County Pumped Storage Hydroelectric Project is the biggest engineering feat in the world—on a small scale," he said, throwing around technical terms like megawatt and cubic feet per second. Wood explained the economic efficiency and environmental advantages of storing power in the uphill reservoir for use during peak-demand periods. He explained the need for power in Chicago, Detroit, and Dayton. Furthermore, he said, "Building the dam would keep down electric costs for customers in Virginia."

A power-company economist explained that the benefit to state and national economies would outweigh any local costs if they built the dams. From his point of view, agriculture along Jack Creek contributed nothing to the gross national product or to national security. The lack of capital improvements on the primitive farms did not enhance the state tax base. Bottom line: People in McDowell did not earn much money, and they did not spend it.

When the power-company speakers finished, Gladys attacked the state for supporting the dams just to increase the taxes paid to them on over-engineered piles of concrete. Monuments to greed and power with built-in obsolescence, she called the dams. She said, "CUPCO would use four units of power pushing water uphill to get three units of power when if flows down, a net loss rather than a gain of power."

Then the chairman called Bill Kelly, the real-estate salesman from Jackson, who had driven to Richmond in his own Jeep instead of riding the bus. As he ranted and raved, telling the committee that they had no legal right to take his land without compensation, Grace feared he was alienating the sympathies of the State Senate committee.

Then Marlow Riley stood, a pompous white-haired lawyer in Jackson, who had ridden with Bill. As he rambled on about loving his view of the creek, she worried he would put everyone to sleep. Then Marlow burst into tears, "Why do we have to lose our homes to supply power for people in Ohio?" He continued sobbing until Bill pulled him down. Grace figured the three-piece-suit attorneys could blow Marlow out of the water if they ever came to logical arguments. She was genuinely sorry that Amos wasn't there to say his piece about chaining himself to a tree as the water was rising.

Dennis described the valley's geologic value. "Jack Creek is a unique field site where I can show my students twelve geologic ages within one mile. A place so fine, remote but accessible, magnificent scenery, rapids, and water quality. You want to build two reservoirs that will resemble the Badlands, with high mud banks. You'll turn a paradise into a moonscape."

Emma addressed the ecological diversity of the forest and the streams, a topic Sam would have covered if he had been there. Then it was Grace's turn to speak. She was afraid she would curse like Jim or cry like Marlow.

"Maybe Jack Creek isn't a place for rare species, geysers, or volcanoes," Grace started. "But this valley is a model of human ecology where each individual is a member of the community. People live together in a balance that doesn't consume our scant resources. We look after our ginseng, our grandparents, and simple folk. If eighty-nine-year-old Luther Morrissey doesn't show up to buy his RC Cola every other day at Mrs. Huffman's store, someone goes up to check on him. Fred Swope, born brain damaged, lives in his own house with a color TV to watch and plays games for free at the County Fair." Was she reaching the committee; were they even listening?

"We farm our land in droughts and floods alike without asking federal assistance. This cost/benefit equation is sideways. Folks in McDowell ask for little from government but to leave us alone. We don't need a dam because we don't use air conditioning. You may think I'm just a kid, but I speak from my heart because I love my father's land and want to keep the heritage he left me."

She ended, "How can we quantify quality of life? Aldo Leopold said in *Sand County Almanac*, 'A thing is right if it tends to preserve the integrity, stability, and beauty of the biotic community.' On Jack Creek, we are a self-sustaining, living community. Senators of the General Assembly, please declare Jack Creek a scenic river."

After Grace spoke, others from McDowell asked to be recognized, if only to add, "I want to live where my grandmother lived, too," or "I like Jack Creek just the way it is." "If I need a hickory tree for the back of a chair, I can go out my backdoor and cut it," Charlie Dorset said.

177

Hilda Huffman said, "I can live just fine without electricity. Go ahead and cut the power line to Jack Creek Valley, if you'll just leave us alone. People in McDowell live like the rest of America would like to live, but cities are spoiled because people do not work their land and tend animals with their families. We're healthier because we eat vegetables we plant in soil where we know there are no chemicals. We drink milk from cows we know and eat eggs from chickens we call by name. City people squander electricity to keep them company."

White-haired Emily Puffenbarger tottered, but spoke fiercely. "Chief Seattle said, 'The shining water that moves in the streams and rivers is not just water but the blood of our ancestors. If we sell you our land, you must remember that it is sacred. . . . Every hillside, every valley, every clearing and wood, is holy in the memory and experience of my people.'" Emily paused. "If I have to move from my family land, I'll just up and die before I'd move."

When Ruby rose to speak, Grace had no idea what she was going to say. "I've been studying my Bible patiently to understand the new science that Sam Bennett tells me about ocean fossils on top of Potter Mountain. His stories of geologic upheavals do settle with my Bible reading, when I re-consider Psalm number 104:

"*Bless the Lord, O my soul. Thou didst set the earth on its foundations, so that it should never be shaken. Thou didst cover it with the deep as with a garment; the waters stood above the mountains. At thy rebuke they fled* (that is the waters fled)*: at the sound of thy thunder they took to flight. The mountains rose, the valleys sank down to the place which thou didst appoint for them. Thou didst set a bound which the waters should not pass, so that they might not again cover the earth.*

"Sounds to me that the Lord determined to keep Jack Creek's water within its own bank. What I read into this passage confirms both what the scientists say and my own faith. Yes indeed, the sea did cover McDowell County millions of years ago. The sea receded, and the mountains rose—Bluff to the west and Potter to the east—to form Jack Creek Valley in a way that the Lord and we, his children, like very much. Let me repeat: Psalm 104 says, '*Thou*

178

didst set a bound which the waters shall not pass, so that they might not again cover the earth.' Any manmade dam would be a blasphemy." Ruby's wisdom and eloquence moved Grace.

Todd, the river lobbyist, summed up for the scenic-river supporters. "It seems to me every Virginian would want a grandmother's homeplace along Jack Creek. You shouldn't sacrifice the quality of life in this rare community to subsidize runaway materialism in northern industrial cities."

As the chairman closed the hearing, Grace could not guess which way the committee would vote. The federal government would hold other hearings during the EIS process for the federal license. However, state declaration of a scenic river would be the easiest, swiftest way to stop the dam. She would call Gladys for the decision that night after the bus returned to Jackson.

Since few people from McDowell had been to Richmond, they wanted to eat and shop before the bus left. Some opened their picnic lunches in the Capitol Square. Others stopped in the S&W cafeteria. Grace led a group the three blocks on Franklin Street to Miller and Rhoads. Most of the ladies never got beyond the first-floor scarves, handbags, jewelry, and gourmet food.

One teenage girl got her face all made-up at a cosmetic counter. Her mother said, "All right, you can wear that gunk home on the bus, but you better wash your face before your father sees you." Others found party gowns and lingerie, pots and pans, sheets and towels. They were sightseeing instead of shopping. Pictures in the Sears catalogue were more familiar to them than the real items.

Ruby would not ride the escalator, so Grace found the elevator to the fourth floor. In the Tea Room, she had reserved a table next to the runway so Ruby could watch the fashion show and hear Eddie Weaver play show tunes on his organ.

When all stragglers boarded the bus at the corner by Loew's Theatre between Miller & Rhoads and Thalhimers, Grace directed the driver down Monument Avenue. Helen Brown, the history teacher, gave a Civil War lesson as they passed equestrian statues of Robert E. Lee, Jeb Stuart, and Stonewall Jackson. Grace told them

179

that bees had once filled Lee's bronze horse with honey, and someone had to drill a hole in the belly to drain it.

From Jared's late-night rambles, Grace knew the Confederate generals' last words. After being wounded by his own troops, before he died, Stonewall Jackson said, "Come let us cross this deep river and rest in the shade of the trees." The McDowell county seat, the only town, was named after Stonewall Jackson.

Grace told the bus, "Defending the outer ring of defenses, Jeb Stuart said, 'We must protect the ladies of Richmond.'"

Ruby declared it was a pity that women should be helpless to defend themselves.

26

From what Grace could piece together later from Sam's field notes, he was close to finding the elusive endangered guppy he decided was most likely in the Jack Creek watershed. He hoped he had found the right place at the waterfall. The falls would be a perfect barrier to migration downstream, and the headwater of the stream in the James River watershed was 500 meters from the headwaters of the Potomac.

Regardless of the rain, Sam would have worked until dark wading the stream upriver of the waterfall. When he tried to start his bus, the ignition, temperamental in damp weather, did not turn over the engine. Since it was cold, wet, and dark, he decided to sleep in the bus and to try the engine in the morning, early enough to intercept the bus in Jackson.

Sam slept well all night, but his VW would not start in the morning. Maybe he really had found a red-bellied mountain dace, the endangered species that he wanted to display at the scenic-river hearing. Sam knew Grace scolded him about missing deadlines.

That morning Sam would have considered the distance from Headwaters to Jackson too far to walk. As much as Sam liked wading rivers, Grace reminded herself, he hated getting wet in the rain. He would have figured he could paddle down the narrow stream, which was higher than usual after the week's rain, faster than he could walk out. When he reached a bridge, he could hitchhike to Richmond for the hearing.

When she drove up later to look at the waterfall, she saw that the river downstream veered away from the road. She reconstructed his motives and actions. Late and too lazy to portage, Sam thought he could save time. Ordinarily safety conscious, Sam had cut corners because he was rushing, because he did not want to disappoint Grace. But he had told her in West Virginia that he was cautious when he worked alone.

But, apparently, Sam had run the little waterfall without

scouting the chute. He thought he could judge the drop well enough from above. He stood in his boat to pick a channel through the rocks. In the pre-dawn dusk he could not see from above that the waterfall was just the length of his boat.

As he crested the waterfall, he may have sensed the danger and felt a tinge of panic. There were only rocks to his left or right. Like a parabola drawn earthward by gravity on its falling curve, the canoe dropped. All this took a second.

The boat stopped abruptly at a 45-degree angle, its bow jammed between rubble at the base of the waterfall and a boulder at the top. The rapid had only an eight or ten-foot drop, but was just fifteen feet long, so that it could catch and hold a boat.

Momentum threw Sam forward, and as he must have tried to jump out, he caught his left leg between the center thwart, the Styrofoam flotation, and the side of the boat. He was stuck in the boat, just as the boat was stuck in the rapid.

Like a rooster's feather, water washed over his back, shoulders, and head, so that he could breathe by straining up his neck and back to create an air pocket. Grace knew Sam had a methodical approach to solving problems. He would not have panicked.

Standing on the bank, she could not imagine his red canoe, stuck under the frothy stream of white water. No one could have seen the boat under the waterfall. Sam would have calmly reviewed his situation. He slid his right hand out to gauge the depth of the water over his back and estimate its temperature.

Someone walking along the bank early that morning might have been surprised to see a hand emerge from the waterfall just as the hand rose from the lake to retrieve King Arthur's sword Excalibur.

Sam knew the water was too cold for him to wait long for someone to find him. He had to figure a way to get free. When the canoe jammed and he slid forward, he had sprained his left shoulder. Perhaps he knew he would tire quickly as the water chilled his body. Therefore, he had angled his paddle under his chest so that he could lean on it and keep breathing. The paddle emerged slightly from the jet of water, just visible to an observant eye.

Amos had once threatened to chain himself to a rock if they proceeded with flooding the valley, and Grace thought Amos was being melodramatic. Sam getting caught underwater was no joke.

After Amos got off the bus before dawn, he had looked for the old green VW bus along roads that paralleled streams. After milking time, he stopped at the general store to find others to help. Cobb Currie drove so Amos and Nether Cline could look. Two other truckloads went up into the mountains to search other streams.

When they found the VW bus without a canoe on the rack on the logging road above the Dorset farm, Nether walked upstream. But Amos knew Sam always carried his canoe on the roof, so he walked down one bank of the stream and Cobb Currie walked the other.

Just a ways downstream Amos sensed a presence and glancing quickly, he thought he saw a hand for a few seconds sticking out of the waterfall. Looking closer, he could see the tip of a paddle barely emerging from the froth of whitewater, blown spumy by the rocks. Amos, who could not swim, clambered into the deep pool at the base of the waterfall and caught sight of the red canoe. Amos could not scramble up the waterfall to get to Sam in the boat. Cobb, standing on the rocks at the top of the fall, could not get down. They shoved the bow and stern of the boat as best they could.

Working together, Amos and Cobb could not budge the boat, weighing a thousand pounds full of water, with the waterfall continually flowing into it. They two struggled, exhausted, until Nether came along and noticed the rope from the bow of the boat floating in the pool below the waterfall. Pulling on it did not free the boat. They needed more leverage. Amos would not leave the boat with Sam in it.

Nether ran back to the VW to search for a coil of rope. They tied the long rope to the boat's bowline, wrapped it around a tree on the bank, and all three pulled. Maybe the stream's water level had gradually lowered after discharging the night's rain. Maybe they had superhuman strength, but the three men freed the boat. As the boat slid loose, tipped and wallowed down the waterfall, Amos jumped into the pool again to recover Sam.

Sam was unconscious, hyperthermic from two or three hours in the cold water. The three men carried him to shore. Sam could not have moved his hand to signal. Amos figured it was the oar he saw. He tried mouth-to-mouth resuscitation on Sam, for a long time, until the other two men gently persuaded him to drive his body to the county doctor.

If there had been a red-bellied mountain dace in a Ball jar or a plastic bag, it had washed out when the canoe broached.

As Grace stood above the waterfall trying to understand why Sam had died like her father, a kingfisher chitter-chittered down the stream. The bird flew closer to her to rest on a branch above the roar of the waterfall.

"Oh kingfisher, only in myths can you restore dead kings."

27

In Quaker Meeting, as spirit covers those who are waiting, frequently the same idea comes to several people, and one may feel moved to voice the message out of the silence. When another person says out loud exactly what you are thinking, a newcomer may think it coincidental or uncanny. But Quakers are accustomed to synchronicity.

When ninety, maybe a hundred people gathered to remember Sam in the yellow frame house of the Charlottesville Friends Meeting, they shared an electricity of common purpose.

"We Friends believe there is a spark of Divine Presence in each person," Chester, the clerk of Meeting, said as the gathering settled in silence. "We wish to celebrate Sam Bennett's life, rather than mourn his death."

Grace wanted to avoid any scene of public grief, but Ruby convinced her to drive to this Quaker memorial service. People overflowed from the main meeting room onto chairs set up in the kitchen and on the porch. Some stood in the yard by the open windows. Grace could recognize members of the Quaker meeting and students from the Environmental Sciences department amid bright colors of clothing. She was glad to see Emma Coleman among unfamiliar faces.

Sam was buried the day before, the first of September, in Augusta, Georgia. Harry Benton had handled the arrangements, as he handled all business for Ruby and Amos. Grace had found Mr. Bennett's number through directory assistance and called him late the night after the hearing. At Ruby's suggestion, Grace offered that Sam could be buried in the Brewer's Notch graveyard, next to her father, where she and Ruby expected to be buried. She didn't consider that the water would rise if the dam were built. However, Mr. Bennett told Grace he wanted to bury Sam next to his own mother.

Grace did not go to Augusta to meet Sam's father, and he did not come to Charlottesville. He told her matter-of-factly to give his son's things to the Environmental Sciences Department or to any of his friends. She called Mark and Jay to divide up his clothes, books, and records. Amos would get his banjo. That and his abandoned boat were all he had of value.

Value. Grace could not settle into the silence. She was anxious and angry with Sam for leaving. After ten minutes, a round, red-cheeked woman with a twist of gray hair stood to say: "At our Christmas dinner last year, when we broke into groups to talk about giving, Sam slipped into my kitchen and washed dishes for thirty people. When we went to clean up, he had just finished. He's the first man I ever asked for one of his recipes, but Sam told me he took what ingredients happened his way. Sam had a gift for enjoying."

Grace had feared that committing to a relationship meant sacrificing her own growth. She wondered if she had been too selfish, fighting the dam rather than paying closer attention to Sam. She felt guilty she had not done enough to prevent him from paddling alone.

Speaking from the corner came a man's voice, "An accident is no one's fault. But what I would give to be able to save Sam." Grace looked up. The speaker was Pete Steer, his canoeing buddy. They prided themselves on paddling most every river in Virginia together. Pete finished, "Because Sam accepted his goof-ups, he looked comfortable."

Next, Jay from Environmental Sciences spoke. "We wear tropical shirts to protest our outrage, just as Sam protested conformity." In a row were six students, young men and women, in gaudy print shirts. "We didn't know if Quakers would wear black for a funeral, but Sam was a colorful Quaker. He would have hated black." Jay choked up.

Silence offered Grace no consolation. She felt sullen, miserly with her mourning, reluctant to reduce her pain, to accept his death as God's will. She did not plan to speak.

"Sam's faith in ecology comforts me now." This was Wendy,

stringy blonde hair and raw-skinned, the woman professor who advised Sam. "He saw the rightness of every living thing, the rightness of whatever happens, good or bad as it may appear to us anthropocentric humans." Her northern accent was about as opposite as possible from his Georgia drawl. "Sam was a systems thinker," Wendy said. "He saw the big picture. Sam put his heart into his work."

After an interval, another woman spoke, "Sam made us all feel loved and generously received our love. In his absence, I worry whom I can spoil now, but he would tell me, 'Be kind to each other.' For my own sense of loneliness, I am sorry he left us so early. Tell you one thing, that boy could not carry a tune in a bucket."

Out of the silence, a man chuckled. His laughter disturbed Grace as irreverent. "Sam put a skunk in my car the night before I got married. I don't know who was more indignant—me or the skunk. I admit I was full of vanity that Sam cured."

A boy stood, about fourteen years old, a high school athlete. "Sam was my Boy Scout leader." Grace did not know he led a scout troupe. "Facing death is like the sunset last night. The sun just below the horizon edged clouds with light. After-life must be something like those bright clouds."

"Sam has let me down," an old man said in good humor, then serious. "I was counting on his tricks to keep me young, and now he's gone off before me."

Ruby stood and spoke, "Surely there's a connection. Don't begrudge age or the cold; we need frost to make the sap rise in sugar maple trees." Grace knew Ruby had been wary of the Quaker meeting without ministers. She was the only one in her own Methodist church and in the valley who didn't see herself as a minister. "Don't begrudge death either, as it is a gathering to God." Grace remembered Ruby's story about the hermit on the mountain.

Emma Coleman said, "Sam honored life in all creatures around him. After I refused chemo, I have been living with pain from cancer for two years, more easily with Sam's teasing. He brought me Wendell Berry's poem: 'I come into the peace of wild things who do not tax their lives with forethought of grief.' Of anybody I've met, Sam did not tax his life with grief—or much forethought either." Someone snorted, then was quiet.

Emma finished, "Sam was ageless and made us all feel forever young. And now he'll never grow old. We who suffer private grief can take comfort with this community of friends." Grace wanted her grief to hurt the worst. She was the guiltiest.

Grace couldn't get the gospel lyrics out of her mind, "Never grow old, never grow old, in a land where we'll never grow old." She started to hum to herself, then shushed.

As comfort to fill her mind, to herself Grace recited the Twenty-third Psalm, "He makes me to lie down in green pastures. He leads me beside the still waters," repeating these lines over and over. Green pastures and still waters, she reflected on the irony of still waters. What kind of God would let Sam get stuck underwater?

Emma and Ruby had said the same thing about faith. Grace finished the psalm in her mind, until "I will dwell in the house of the Lord forever." Which house? She had spent the first half of her life in the farmhouse, the second part in Eleanor's Richmond house. Maybe the yellow clapboard Quaker meetinghouse in Charlottesville was a home where Grace could belong in the decade of her twenties. "The house of the Lord" comforted her. In this yellow house, embracing doubt as she found more questions than answers, she might strengthen her faith. She would remember how to pray, as she had done in her attic bedroom when her father had tucked her in.

Grace remembered one night at the farmhouse when she was waiting for Sam. She sat on the doorsill on the front porch, happy to wait for him for once, because she savored belonging with someone. That night she had prayed, Don't ever let Sam become a memory. She felt already that so many people had left her life. She didn't mean just her father, but friends in elementary school when she moved to Richmond, and friends she had lost along the way after sixth grade.

In the doorway that night, she had prayed, Let me always love Sam as I do now. Unconsciously Grace found that she was standing, moved to speak.

"When I asked what Sam wanted to be reincarnated as, for me I said, 'Otter,' and he said 'October.' So I'll expect him back every time the air tastes crisp, when the first frost turns leaves orange, to hurry the harvest. I had difficulty accepting that Sam was not concerned with being on time. He taught me the value of slowing time. Sam will come back each October to help the creatures like him who played all summer prepare for winter." Grace sat down content that Sam was her healthy other half, who would continue to influence her.

A clear soprano started singing "Amazing Grace," resounding in the small meeting room. Voices joined in harmony. She opened her mouth to sing, but her heart moved up and closed her throat. She could not sing without crying.

Sam is the first man I have trusted since my father, Grace thought. Her chest expanded as if her heart were getting bigger, easing the burden of grief. Her feeling deepened to love, so grief turned to joy. The tightness in her throat rose, and a flush covered her cheeks and forehead. Grace began to cry, like rain that's necessary after planting. Ruby handed her a handkerchief and clutched her hand.

Grace did not finish grieving in that hour of Quaker memorial service. But in telling her story, forgiving her own gracelessness, claiming her name and memories, raising her voice, she began slowly to understand.

When Grace and Ruby had returned to the farm from the hearing in Richmond a week earlier, Amos told how he found the canoe caught in the stream.

"Sam was still holding on to his paddle just like he planned to keep moving," Amos sobbed. "I could not save Sam from drowning, anymore than I could save your father."

Grace could not console Amos then, but she would go back to comfort him. Like her father, Sam loved the river, music, and fishing. They were both impetuous, goofy, twinkling eyes full of mischief and loyalty. Sam had given her a chance to recognize her father, and Amos had seen that resemblance too.

At eighteen, Grace did not release all her fears of marriage and motherhood, of abandoning or being abandoned. The running river, cold-water riffles, and skinnydipping pool washed away new and old grief. The spirit of her family and homeplace stayed alive in her songs and stories.

Grace thanked whatever power had shared Sam with her. He believed she was worth something and left her to test his lesson. It was not her fault for loving her father so much that he had died, anymore than it was her fault Sam died.

28

Yellow gold—the color of glory. Yellow, red, and orange swathes of color covered the far hillside, with some few leaves still spring green. Firs stayed evergreen. Grace picked a sprig of hemlock, crushed it pungent between her fingertips, and held it to her nose. That afternoon she had visited Sally Bee's children, growing big fast. Grace put the sprig of hemlock in her parka pocket to carry with her and touched the pottery shard, still there, she had found paddling the creek with Sam.

With no haze, layers of hills in the distance were not blue, but distinct, each separate, and brilliant with fall color before winter winds blew trees bare. The sky was the bluest she could remember and the temperature sharp with chill, so Grace was grateful for the noon sun. Ruby had resumed cooking on the woodstove instead of the electric range, keeping the coals smoldering all day to warm the house.

"I'll go fetch Amos for dinner," Grace told Ruby. She walked the long way across the lower pasture to follow the creek north to Amos's cabin. Below, by the pasture, sun sparkled on playful water in a rock garden in the creek.

Inner light was a Quaker image that she liked. In the light and music of the water she recognized Sam's twinkle and her father's laughter—always near her, these men who taught her to let herself be loved. Light on the water was what she owned, more than the land, and intended to share, the light in her, and her faith to see light in every person.

"Amos," Grace yelled as she walked on the front porch of his cabin. The dank little log house always surprised her by its darkness, like an animal's cave. Amos sat inside wearing his gray quilted jacket, because he had started no fire. He usually spent his days outside roaming the woods.

"Amos, I've come to fetch you for dinner," Grace said gently, as she sat in the other chair. "I brought you Sam's banjo."

"I'm no musician."

"You can take lessons from Farley."

Walking along the woods path back to the farm, a flash of gaudy pink and red caught her eye. "What is this, Amos?" Trained by him, she did not pick the flower, but held the branch so Amos could identify it. A fuchsia pink husk cracked open to reveal three neon orange fruits.

"What is this shrub's name?" Grace asked.

"I can't tell you." Amos was buried in his own grief, and she was trying to reach him.

"Please, Amos, it's so amazing," she said.

"Some call it strawberry bush," he said, "but up here we call it Hearts 'a Bursting."

"My heart's going to heal, Amos, and yours will too." Silent companionship comforted them both as they walked.

Grace could not by herself save her father or Sam. But she had grown a bigger heart. At Sam's memorial, she had felt her heart stretch to fill her chest.

What Grace had learned—as Kenneth Boulding, the Quaker economist who was a poet, wrote—"So life is love, and love the end must be."

"Amos, do you have any regrets? Why didn't you ever marry Ruby?" Grace had never pried before, but always wondered why the two old friends had not paired off.

"We were cousins," Amos answered easily.

"Naw, you're only cousins by marriage," she said, "and she does not care that you are younger than she is."

"I reckon," he said, "because I did not have any land of my own, and she didn't really either, because Tom owned this land."

"But you have everybody's land to walk on," she said. "Like Thoreau enjoyed the woods he surveyed better than the farmers who owned them. Whoever owns something is who loves it most. I didn't own my family land until this summer, and you know it better than I do."

"What about the dam?" Amos asked. "With all the

commotion I forgot to ask." He did not say Sam drowning and his funeral.

"The state committee turned down the scenic-river proposal for Jack Creek. We have lost the first round, so the federal government will prepare an environmental impact statement for the project, and there will be more hearings next year in Richmond or Washington. We will have other chances to protest."

Grace had a feeling they would not win by fighting for the land and agonizing over their opponents' power and greed. Rather their claims to Jack Creek would be stronger if they continued living on the land as they always had—growing vegetables, tending animals, making crafts, and minding neighbors and kin. As the Quakers say, let your lives speak.

When Grace had first arrived on the creek in the spring, she was not a social snob like her mother, but was nevertheless an elitist. She thought the only value people had was their education and intellect. She had feared close-minded rural farmers with conservative politics, but she met folks with open minds and rich hearts.

When Grace started classes that fall at the University in Charlottesville, instead of Sweet Briar, she spent weekends with Ruby. She was preparing to teach as her father had done. *Jess like her Daddy.* Both Ruby and Amos had shared their gifts of wisdom with Grace. With them, she could love Sam and survive losing him. She could even survive the dam, but she would not give up living on the land until they all had to move.

The new environmental laws of the 1970s could not save the valley, or her family's century farm—the Environmental Policy Act, the Clean Water Act, the Endangered Species Act. Finally, the government approved the dam, then delayed because of decreased demand for electricity. Some people along the creek moved when the power company started chopping trees in the National Forest, but then it postponed construction for two years because of financial complications.

For two years after Grace graduated from college, she lived with Ruby and taught in the McDowell County schools. One by one, families left Jack Creek Valley, dispersed to split-levels in subdivisions. Neighbors lost their interdependent community where one family raised chickens and bartered eggs for milk; one man was a mechanic and another mowed.

When Ruby was not yet sixty, she climbed to the top of Bluff Mountain one last time to settle with her God, rather than move from Jack Creek Valley. She had never lived anywhere else. Ruby was buried at Brewer's Notch Methodist Church. The congregation decided not to move any bodies in the church graveyard, but to let them lie with their kin under the reservoir.

Grace felt comfort: *"Remember that the river flows from the mountain to the sea, and that it will then evaporate, form into clouds, and come back as rain to fill the river again."*

When the water started to rise, Amos moved up the hollow to live with Farley. The two rivals stopped competing and started to cooperate, since no other neighbors were left. When Grace came to visit every few weeks, walking half a mile over the divide from Route 250 to their cabin, they were getting older and older, but never looked any different to her. Must be because they drink Farley's magic spring water, she thought.

"Amos, let's go dig some ginseng," Grace said, as they climbed a knoll to overlook where her father's orchard had been, above the still slowly-rising water of the reservoir.

"I sold a few roots this month, but I can show you some plants before the frost kills the leaves." Amos led her to one of his patches hidden from the path.

The three sets of five leaves were bronze, the berries red. Grace knelt and brushed dirt and rocks from the base of a plant. She dug with her fingers, tugged gently and steadily on the triple stalks, freeing the plant from soil and rock, until she pulled up a gnarled root, three inches long, like a carrot, with two legs. Not quite like a man's whole body.

"Oh, that's a fine valuable piece," Amos said. "It will bring a pretty price. The Chinese like the roots all twisted from growing in rocky ground. They say there's more spiritual power if it grows in a difficult place."

"No, Amos, we're not going to sell this root," Grace said clearly, standing to face him. "We're going to brew ginseng tea and drink it together, you and me, because I need you to live a long time, until I have a daughter for you to teach to dance."

Acknowledgments

Gratitude for residencies at Virginia Center for the Creative Arts at Sweet Briar and Auvillar, France; Bread Loaf, Vermont Studio Center, and a Cape Cod Dune Shack. And for fellowships from National Endowment for the Humanities, National Science Foundation, Fulbright, North Carolina Arts Council, American Association of University Women. I have learned about craft from writers in workshops I took and taught. Thanks to careful readers: Janet Bellin, Ella and Jean Carter, Emily Yelton Ausband, Woody Hobbs, and Jeff Schmidt. Thanks to my Beaufort Writing Group critique community and to my other brothers.

Kakapo Press publishes place-based books.

Photo of kākāpō *by Sabine Bernert*
Crown © Department of Conservation Te Papa Atawhai
http://kakaporecovery.org.nz/donate/

About the Author

As developmental editor, **SUSAN SCHMIDT** polishes science and history books, novels, and memoirs—with the same mindfulness as pruning apple trees. She has worked as sailboat captain, science-policy analyst, and professor of literature and environmental decision-making. She has a doctorate in American literature and a Masters in Environmental Sciences.

To witness natural diversity, she walked the Camino de Santiago, Cornwall Coastal Path, Scottish Highlands, Ring of Kerry, and Appalachian Trail; surveyed birds in Kenya and Ecuador; paddled most of Virginia's rivers, Prince William Sound, and Milford Sound; and delivered sailboats to the West Indies. Her homeplace is the Chesapeake Bay in Virginia, and her homeport is Beaufort, North Carolina, where she walks beaches with her Boykin Spaniel.

Susan wrote *Landfall Along the Chesapeake, In the Wake of Captain John Smith,* an ecological history and boat adventure, and *Salt Runs in My Blood,* a poetry book about bright parrots, big trout, glaciers, peach pie, old loves, Celtic ancestry, gales at sea, and learning to navigate.

susu@susanschmidt.net
www.susanschmidt.net

38596337R00124

Made in the USA
Charleston, SC
14 February 2015